I WANT TO
EAT
PASTA

I WANT TO
EAT
PASTA

OVER 90 EASY PASTA RECIPES USING 10 INGREDIENTS OR LESS

Giovanna Torrico

Photography Lisa Linder

Hardie Grant

NORTH AMERICA

CONTENTS

INTRODUCTION

Pasta is loved all over the world, but for Italians, pasta is more than just food. It is a symbol of national pride; everyone shares a profound interest in pasta and it brings back memories of when we were children and sharing a big family Sunday lunch where pasta was the highlight.

Pasta is also magic. It consists of just two ingredients: flour and water or egg, which are kneaded together, worked, and left to dry to create the best comfort food in the world.

In this book I have just used dried pasta as this is the most widely available option. However, don't think that dried pasta is all the same, just branded differently, because this is not the case. When choosing dried pasta, try to find trafilata al bronzo, or "bronze-cut" pasta. This pasta is passed through bronze dies (metal plates) to give it a rougher consistency and a porous texture to help it hold more of the sauce accompanying it. I always recommend buying the highest-quality variety where possible. La Molisana is one of my favorite brands.

There are many advantages of using dried pasta but one of the main ones is speed. You can easily make delicious meals in the time it takes to boil the water and cook the pasta. Another advantage is its versatility, as there is a pasta dish for every occasion, from a quick dinner of Cacio e Pepe (page 22), to a lazy Sunday meal with friends sharing a decadent Lasagna (page 159) or Rigatoni Cake (page 147).

THE ITALIAN PANTRY

If you have a bag of dried pasta in your pantry, you can create a simple meal with just a few added ingredients. Here is a list of the ideal ingredients to keep in your kitchen so you are ready to cook. Italian-style cooking relies on the quality of the ingredients used, so try to opt for the best quality you can get.

REFRIGERATOR INGREDIENTS

1. Fresh vegetables and herbs
2. Butter
3. Pancetta
4. Hard cheese, such as Parmigiano Reggiano, or ricotta salata
5. Olives
6. Lemons
7. Eggs

PANTRY ESSENTIALS

1. Extra-virgin olive oil
2. Tinned fish preserved in olive oil, including anchovies, tuna, and sardines
3. Canned chopped, whole, or sundried tomatoes
4. Precooked jarred and canned legumes, such as beans, chickpeas, and lentils
5. Strained pureed tomatoes (passata)
6. Spices
7. Mixed dried wild mushrooms
8. Nuts
9. Salt and black pepper
10. Breadcrumbs
11. Capers
12. Garlic and onions
13. Wine

COOKING PASTA

As a general rule, use 4¼ cups (1L) of water for 3½ ounces (100g) dried pasta and ¼ ounce (7–10g) of coarse sea salt (it seems a lot but only a tiny amount will be absorbed by the pasta).

Fill a large saucepan with cold water, cover with a lid, and bring to a boil. Add the salt and when the water is boiling, add the pasta.

Follow the cooking times on the package, but try a piece of pasta 1 or 2 minutes before the end of cooking to see if it's done. The Italians like pasta al dente ("to the tooth"), which means that it should be firm and have a slight resistance when you bite it. Lift the pasta with tongs or drain through a colander, holding back a little of the cooking water to either loosen up the sauce or to finish cooking the pasta in the sauce.

HOW TO MAKE SOFFRITTO

MAKES : 10½ OUNCES (300G)
PREP : 5 MINS
COOK : 5 MINS

INGREDIENTS

¼ cup (60ml) oil

3½ ounces (100g) each minced onion, carrot, and celery

1 garlic cloves, crushed (optional)

Soffritto is an essential base to most sauces. It gives the sauce a characteristic taste and can turn a dish into something special.

1. Heat the butter or oil in a pan over low heat, add the vegetables and garlic (if using), and sauté for 10 minutes, or until golden. Do not let the soffritto burn or brown. Continue with the recipe.

To freeze, chop the vegetables, lay them out on a large baking sheet and freeze until frozen, then transfer to a freezer proof bag and store for up to four months. You can cook directly from frozen.

PASTA SHAPES—THE ART OF PASTA

There are so many different pasta shapes and sauces in every corner of Italy, reflecting the particular region and produce available. Classifying pasta shapes is not an exact science as some can belong to more than one category. In this book, I have divided the pasta shapes into four main groups.

PASTINA, VERY SMALL PASTA: Generally cooked in broths and eaten with a spoon.

PASTA CORTA, SHORT PASTA: Rigatoni, orecchiette, penne, fusilli, etc.

PASTA LUNGA, LONG PASTA: Spaghetti, tagliatelle, fettuccine, pappardelle.

PASTA RIPIENA, FILLED PASTA: Ravioli, tortellini, cannelloni, and lasagna.

PAIRING PASTA SHAPES WITH SAUCES

There are a couple of points to consider when matching pasta shapes with particular sauces. First, think about the texture and surface of the pasta: even the densest sauce will struggle if there is nothing to cling to. Bronze-cut pasta has a better texture. It is rough like sandpaper and porous, which enables it to hold the sauce.

Hollow shapes such as rigatoni or penne hold the sauce. Shells and twisted forms like fusilli naturally catch the condiments. Tiny shapes are good in broths or soups. Long pasta is best with a seafood or creamy sauce.

Long-ribboned pasta such as tagliatelle are perfect paired with a porcini mushroom sauce or hearty ragù.

A GUIDE TO PASTA SHAPES

PASTINA (SMALL)

1.
2.
3.
4.
5.

PASTA CORTA (SHORT PASTA)

6.
7.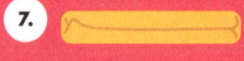
8.
9.
10.
11.
12.

13.
14.
15.
16.
17.
18.
19.
20.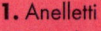

1. Anelletti
2. Conchiglie
3. Ditalini
4. Fregula
5. Orzo
6. Calamarata
7. Casarecce
8. Conchiglioni
9. Fusilli al ferretto
10. Fusilli
11. Gnocchi
12. Cavatappi
13. Mezzi rigatoni
14. Orecchiette
15. Paccheri
16. Penne
17. Rigatoni
18. Tortiglioni
19. Trofie
20. Ziti

PASTA RIPIENA (FILLED PASTA)

PASTA LUNGA (LONG PASTA)

21. Cannelloni
22. Lasagna
23. Ravioli
24. Tortellini
25. Tagliolini

26. Tonnarelli
27. Bucatini
28. Fettuccine
29. Linguine
30. Long Ziti

31. Mafaldine
32. Pappardelle
33. Spaghetti
34. Tagliatelle

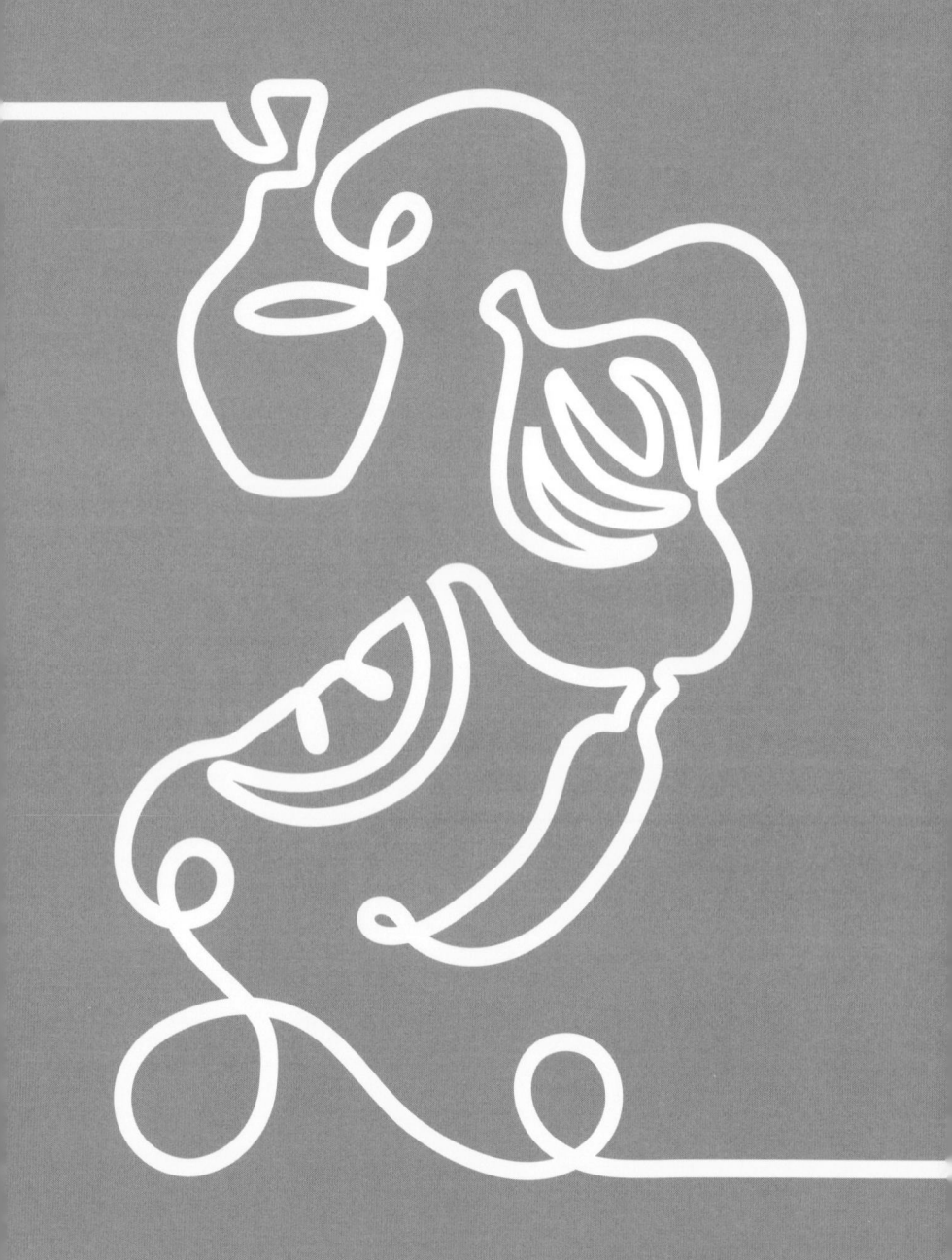

FIVE
INGREDIENTS

PASTA ALLA GENOVESE

SERVES: 4
PREP: 10 MINS
COOK: 180 MINS

INGREDIENTS

¼ cup (60ml) extra-virgin olive oil

10½ ounces (300g) soffritto (page 10)

6 onions, thinly sliced

1 pound (500g) boneless beef chuck roast, trimmed and cut into 3 by 4-inch (7.5 by 10cm) pieces

4 tablespoons white wine

12 ounces (360g) dried ziti

salt and pepper

grated Parmesan cheese, for serving

Genovese sauce is a traditional recipe from Campania, not from Liguria, despite its name. It is a white ragù prepared with beef and onions, which are slowly cooked until they become a delicious puree.

1. Heat the oil in a large saucepan over medium heat, add the soffritto and onions, and sauté for a few minutes. Add the meat, fry for 1 minute, then add the wine and cook for a few minutes. Reduce the heat and let simmer for 3 hours, or until the sauce thickens, stirring occasionally and adding some hot water, if necessary. Season to taste.

2. Bring a large saucepan of water to a boil, add salt, then add the pasta and cook for 1 minute less than the package directions.

3. Drain the pasta, setting aside 2 tablespoons of the cooking water, and return it to the saucepan. Add the sauce and stir until the pasta is fully coated, adding the reserved cooking water, if necessary. Serve with grated Parmesan.

ORECCHIETTE WITH BROCCOLI

SERVES: 2
PREP: 5 MINS
COOK: 10 MINS

INGREDIENTS

⅓ pound (150g) dried orecchiette

1 small broccoli head, cut into florets and stalk peeled and chopped

2 tablespoons extra-virgin olive oil

1 garlic clove, lightly crushed

½ chile, seeded and finely chopped

salt and pepper

grated Parmesan cheese, for serving

This is a classic dish from Puglia, where the local pasta shape is perfect to catch the broccoli and olive oil, which is found in abundance in this region. Cooking the broccoli with the pasta saves time.

1. Bring a large saucepan of water to a boil, add salt, then add the pasta and cook for 1 minute less than the package directions. When there are 5 minutes left, add the broccoli to the pan.

2. Meanwhile, heat the oil in a large skillet over medium heat, add the crushed garlic and chopped chile, and cook for a few minutes.

3. Drain the pasta and broccoli, setting aside a ladleful of the cooking water, add to the skillet, and cook, shaking and tossing the pan, for another 1 minute, adding a splash of the reserved cooking water, if needed. Season to taste and serve with grated Parmesan.

RIGATONI ALLA NORMA

SERVES: 2
PREP: 30 MINS
COOK: 15 MINS

INGREDIENTS

1 quantity of Fresh Tomato Sauce (page 43)

1 eggplant, cut into ⅓-inch (8mm) slices

Oil, for frying

6 ounces (180g) dried rigatoni

4 tablespoons salted ricotta cheese, grated

salt and pepper

chopped basil, for garnishing

This is the pasta specialty of Catania, a city in Sicily, and is homage to the famous composer Vincenzo Bellini. It is a delicious pasta dish of fried eggplants and salted ricotta.

1. Puree the tomatoes in a food mill to make a smooth sauce. Place the sliced eggplant in a colander, sprinkle with salt, and let drain for 15 minutes. Rinse and pat dry with paper towels.

2. Heat the oil in a skillet over medium heat, add the eggplants, and fry for 1 to 2 minutes. Remove from the pan and drain on paper towels to remove any excess oil.

3. Meanwhile, bring a large saucepan of water to a boil, add salt, then add the pasta and cook for 1 minute less than the package directions.

4. Drain the pasta, setting aside a ladleful of the cooking water. Add the pasta to the sauce and toss until it is well coated adding some of the reserved cooking water. Divide the pasta among serving plates, then add the fried eggplants, grated ricotta, and chopped basil.

CACIO E PEPE

INGREDIENTS

6 ounces (180g) dried tonnarelli or spaghetti

1 teaspoon black peppercorns, lightly crushed

²/₃ cup (100g) grated Pecorino Romano cheese

salt

This famous Roman dish is all about simplicity and quality ingredients as there are only three—pasta, pepper, and pecorino cheese.

1. Bring a large saucepan of water to a boil, add salt, then add the pasta and cook for 2 minutes less than the package directions.

2. Meanwhile, toast the crushed peppercorns in a pan, stirring, over low heat for 1 minute. Add a ladleful of the pasta cooking water and keep the heat low.

3. A couple of minutes before you drain the pasta, place the cheese in a bowl, add a ladleful of the pasta cooking water, and whisk vigorously to make a thick paste.

4. Drain the pasta, setting aside some of the cooking water, and add to the pan with the pepper. Turn off the heat, add the cheese mixture, and toss vigorously until the cheese coats the pasta, adding some of the reserved cooking water, if necessary. Serve immediately.

TAGLIATELLE WITH BOLOGNESE SAUCE

SERVES: 4
PREP: 5 MINS
COOK: 135 MINS

INGREDIENTS

2 tablespoons extra-virgin olive oil

10½ ounces (300g) soffritto (page 10)

1¾ cups (400g) mixed ground beef and pork

¼ cup (60ml) red wine

1¾ cups (400g) strained pureed tomatoes (passata)

12 ounces (360g) dried egg tagliatelle

salt

grated Parmesan cheese, for serving

Bolognese is without a doubt one of the most famous Italian sauces. It is typically added to lasagna, one of the staples of Italian cuisine. Authentic Bolognese is nearly always served with tagliatelle and not spaghetti.

1. Heat the oil in a saucepan over medium heat, add the soffritto, and sauté for about 3 minutes. Add the ground meat and cook until browned, breaking up the meat with a wooden spoon as you stir.

2. Add the wine and stir to remove any bits that have stuck to the bottom of the pan. Once the alcohol has evaporated, add the strained pureed tomatoes and 1 cup (250ml) hot water. Season with salt and cook for 2 hours, stirring occasionally, until the meat is tenderized and all the flavors have intensified.

3. Bring a large saucepan of water to a boil, add salt, then add the pasta and cook for 1 minute less than the package directions. Drain the pasta, setting aside 2 tablespoons of the cooking water, in case the sauce is too thick. Add the pasta to the sauce and slowly mix until well coated. Serve with grated Parmesan.

SPAGHETTI WITH CLAMS

SERVES: 2
PREP: 35 MINS
COOK: 15 MINS

INGREDIENTS

1 pound (500g) small clams

2 tablespoons extra-virgin olive oil

1 garlic clove, crushed

¼ cup (60ml) white wine

6 ounces (180g) dried spaghetti

salt

chopped parsley, for garnishing

Spaghetti with clams is a classic Neapolitan dish. It is a very simple recipe with just a few ingredients, but the end result is a spectacular pasta dish with a wonderful seafood flavor.

1. Wash the clams and let soak in a bowl of salted water for 30 minutes.

2. Bring a large saucepan of water to a boil, add salt, then add the pasta and cook for 2 minutes less than the package directions.

3. Meanwhile, wash and drain the clams. Heat the oil in a large skillet with a lid over medium heat, add the garlic, and cook until fragrant. Add the clams and wine, cover tightly, and shake the pan until the clams open.

4. Drain the pasta and add to the pan with the clams. Toss together for a minute until the pasta is fully coated. Discard any clams that have not opened. Sprinkle with parsley and serve.

CREAMY TROFIE WITH ZUCCHINI

SERVES : 2
PREP : 5 MINS
COOK : 10 MINS

INGREDIENTS

2 tablespoons extra-virgin olive oil

1 garlic clove, lightly crushed

2 small mixed colored zucchini, sliced

6 ounces (180g) dried trofie

½ cup (125g) ricotta cheese

salt and pepper

grated Parmesan cheese, for serving

This dish is very easy, ideal if you are short on time but still want to eat something delicious. Try to use a good-quality ricotta for a delicate and well-balanced sauce.

1. Heat the oil in a skillet, add the garlic, and fry until fragrant. Add the zucchini, a splash of water, and season with salt and pepper. Cook for 5 minutes, then remove the garlic and puree a third of the zucchini in a food processor or blender.

2. Meanwhile, bring a large saucepan of water to a boil, add salt, then add the pasta and cook for 2 minutes less than the package directions.

3. Add the ricotta and zucchini puree to the skillet with the remaining zucchini and add a ladleful of the pasta cooking water.

4. Drain the pasta and add to the pan with the ricotta and zucchini. Stir well for 1 minute to combine, then serve with Parmesan.

FETTUCCINE WITH WHITE RAGÙ

INGREDIENTS

3 tablespoons extra-virgin olive oil

10½ ounces (300g) soffritto (page 10)

1 cup (250g) ground beef

1 cup (250g) ground pork

scant 1 cup (200ml) white wine

1¾ cups (400ml) beef stock

1 bouquet garni with rosemary and bay leaf

6 ounces (180g) dried egg fettuccine

salt

chopped rosemary, for serving

Delicious and tasty, white ragù is considered to be traditional compared to the red version as tomatoes arrived in Italy in the mid-1500s. Perfect for so many recipes, this ragù can also be frozen in containers, so you will always have it on hand. When needed, just thaw it overnight in the refrigerator before using.

1. Heat the oil in a saucepan over medium heat, add the soffritto, and sauté for 3 minutes. Add the ground meat and cook until browned, breaking up the meat with a wooden spoon as you stir.

2. Deglaze the pan with the wine and once the alcohol has evaporated, add the beef stock, and bouquet garni. Season with salt and cook for about 40 minutes, stirring occasionally. Remove and discard the bouquet garni.

3. Bring a large saucepan of water to a boil, add salt, then add the pasta and cook for 1 minute less than the package directions. Drain the pasta, setting aside 2 tablespoons of the cooking water. Add the pasta to the ragù and slowly mix, adding a little of the reserved cooking water, until it is well coated. Serve hot.

BURNT SPAGHETTI

SERVES: 2
PREP: 5 MINS
COOK: 20 MINS

INGREDIENTS

1 cup (250g) strained
pureed tomatoes (passata)

2 tablespoons extra-virgin
olive oil, plus extra
for drizzling

1 garlic clove,
lightly crushed

2 red chiles, finely
chopped

6 ounces (180g)
dried spaghetti

salt and pepper

grated Parmesan cheese,
for serving

Also known as assassin's pasta, the name of
this recipe is said to have come about by the
first person to try it. He was so taken aback
by the ferocious heat of the dish that he
called the chef who invented it a "killer."

1. Bring 1¾ cups (400ml) water and scant 1 cup (200g)
of the strained pureed tomatoes to a boil in a large
saucepan. Season with salt and pepper and let it simmer.

2. Heat the oil in a large cast-iron pan, add the garlic
and chiles, and fry until fragrant. Remove and discard the
garlic, then add the remaining strained pureed tomatoes
to the pan. Spread it evenly over the pan, then add the
spaghetti in an even layer and cook for 2 minutes, letting
it stick to the bottom of the pan.

3. Using a spatula, flip the spaghetti over and cook the
other side for another 2 minutes, before adding a ladleful
of the tomato broth. Carefully stir, then turn the spaghetti
and when all the liquid has been absorbed add another
ladleful. Continue until the pasta is al dente. Obviously,
the pasta must not burn, but the secret is to make the
spaghetti stick to the pan evenly, so that it takes on a
crunchy consistency and a brown color.

4. Divide among plates and serve with grated Parmesan.

TORTELLINI IN BROTH

SERVES: 2 + LEFTOVERS
PREP: 5 MINS
COOK: 2 HOURS 10 MINS

INGREDIENTS

2¼ pounds (1kg) mixed meat (beef shoulder, brisket, and chicken wings)

1 bay leaf

1 onion

1 carrot

1 strip of celery stalk

9 ounces (250g) fresh tortellini

salt

grated Parmesan cheese, for serving

This little delicacy, filled with pork, ham, and Parmesan, from the Emilia-Romagna region is a staple part of the Christmas festive season. Make a big batch of the broth and freeze the leftovers for up to three months in sealed freezer bags or ice-cube trays to add extra flavor to pasta soups.

1. Place all the meat, bay leaf, onion, carrot, and celery in a large saucepan and cover with 12 cups (3L) water. Bring to a boil, reduce the heat, cover with a lid, and simmer for 2 hours, skimming occasionally. Season to taste. After the cooking time, strain the broth, setting the meat aside for another recipe. You should be left with 5 cups (1.2L) broth.

2. Pour 2½ cups (600ml) of the broth into a large saucepan and bring to a boil. Add the tortellini and cook according to the package directions. Serve with grated Parmesan.

SAFFRON TAGLIATELLE WITH SHRIMP

SERVES: 2
PREP: 10 MINS
COOK: 25 MINS

INGREDIENTS

7 ounces (200g) fresh shrimp, head and shells removed, discarding shells but keeping heads

1 large pinch of saffron threads

⅓ pound (150g) dried egg tagliatelle

2 tablespoons extra-virgin olive oil

¼ onion, finely sliced

2 tablespoons butter

salt

Rich and luxurious, this saffron and shrimp tagliatelle is quick and easy, making it perfect for busy weeknights. It is also special enough for impromptu entertaining.

1. Place the shrimp heads in a saucepan with ½ glass of water and 1 teaspoon of salt. Bring to a boil and cook for 15 minutes. Strain the broth, stir in the saffron, and set aside.

2. Meanwhile, bring a large saucepan of water to a boil, add salt, then add the pasta and cook for 1 minute less than the package directions.

3. At the same time, heat the oil in a large skillet over medium heat. Add the onion and sauté for a few minutes. Add the broth and let it reduce for 2 minutes, then add the shrimp and cook for another 5 minutes.

4. Drain the pasta, add to the skillet, and mix and toss with the butter until fully combined. Serve immediately.

TROFIE WITH TOMATO CONFIT AND ARUGULA

SERVES:2
PREP:5 MINS
COOK:25 MINS

Trofie with confit cherry tomatoes and arugula is a simple and perfect pasta dish that you will never get tired of eating.

INGREDIENTS

1½ cups (250g) mixed cherry tomatoes, halved

3 tablespoons extra-virgin olive oil

1 large pinch of dried oregano

1 garlic clove, quartered

6 ounces (180g) dried trofie

⅓ pound (150g) arugula

salt and pepper

grated Parmesan cheese, for serving

1. Preheat the oven to 350°F (180°C).

2. Place the tomatoes on a baking sheet, cut-side up. Season them with the oil, oregano, garlic, and salt and pepper and bake in the oven for about 25 minutes.

3. Meanwhile, bring a large saucepan of water to a boil, add salt, then add the pasta and cook for 1 minute less than the package directions.

4. When the pasta is cooked, drain and return to the saucepan. Add the tomato confit and arugula and mix well to combine. Serve hot with grated Parmesan.

FRESH TOMATO SAUCE

ARRABBIATA

MARINARA

TUNA

TOMATOES FOUR WAYS

FRESH TOMATO SAUCE

SERVES : 2
PREP : 2 MINS
COOK : 12 MINS

Italy is home to around 300 different varieties of tomatoes. They are undoubtedly one of the most important ingredients in Italian cuisine.

INGREDIENTS

¼ cup (60ml) extra-virgin olive oil

1 garlic clove, lightly crushed

1 pound (500g) tomatoes, halved

1 basil sprig

salt

1. Heat the oil in a skillet over medium heat, add the garlic, and cook until fragrant.

2. Add the tomatoes and basil. Season with salt and cook for 10 minutes, or until all the tomatoes have burst. Gently mash the tomatoes with a fork to help release the juice.

ARRABBIATA

Heat ¼ cup (60ml) oil and fry 1 crushed garlic clove. Add 1 (15-ounce / 425g) can crushed tomatoes, then season and cook for 10 minutes.

MARINARA

Heat ¼ cup (60ml) oil and fry ½ diced onion and 1 crushed garlic clove. Add 1 (15-ounce / 425g) can tomatoes and ½ teaspoon dried oregano. Season and cook for 20 minutes.

TUNA

Heat 2 tablespoons oil and fry 1 crushed garlic clove; discard garlic. Add ¼ teaspoon hot pepper flakes,1 (15-ounce / 425g) can tomatoes, 2 (2¾-ounce / 80g) tins tuna in oil, drained and flaked, and 1 tablespoon chopped parsley. Season and cook for 10 minutes.

PENNE WITH CAULIFLOWER RAGÙ

SERVES: 2
PREP: 5 MINS
COOK: 25 MINS

INGREDIENTS

1 small cauliflower, cut into florets and stems into chunks

2 tablespoons extra-virgin olive oil

10½ ounces (300g) soffritto (page 10)

1 cup (250g) strained pureed tomatoes (passata)

1 bouquet garni of rosemary, thyme, parsley

6 ounces (180g) dried penne

salt and pepper

This is a flavorful, full-bodied vegetarian dish and a good alternative to a meat ragù. It is a great way of adding an extra one of your five-a-day.

1. Blitz the cauliflower in a food processor until it is finely broken down. Set aside.

2. Heat the oil in a saucepan over medium heat, add the soffritto, and sauté for 3 minutes. Add the strained pureed tomatoes and bouquet garni, then season with salt and cook for 10 minutes. Add the cauliflower, stir everything together, and cook for another 5 to 8 minutes. Remove and discard the bouquet garni when it is ready.

3. Meanwhile, bring a large saucepan of water to a boil, add salt, then add the pasta and cook for 2 minutes less than the package directions. Drain the pasta, setting aside 2 tablespoons of the cooking water. Add the pasta to the sauce and slowly mix until it is well coated, adding the reserved cooking water, if necessary. Season to taste with pepper and serve.

PASTA WITH TUNA AND BALSAMIC VINEGAR

SERVES: 2
PREP: 5 MINS
COOK: 15 MINS

INGREDIENTS

6 ounces (180g) dried fusilli al ferretto

2 tablespoons extra-virgin olive oil

1 (3½-ounce / 100g) fresh tuna steak, diced

½ cup (100g) mixed colored cherry tomatoes, halved

4 ounces (120g) arugula, chopped

1 tablespoon balsamic vinegar

salt and pepper

This is a quick, tasty, and colorful dish. The fresh tuna is lightly seared and the balsamic vinegar has a light and delicately sharp taste, which brings the perfect balance of flavors to this recipe.

1. Bring a large saucepan of water to a boil, add salt, then add the pasta, and cook for 1 minute less than the package directions.

2. Meanwhile, heat the oil in a skillet over medium heat, add the tuna, and cook for 5 minutes. Season with salt and pepper and set aside.

3. Add the tomatoes and arugula to a bowl and season with salt, pepper, and the vinegar.

4. Drain the pasta and add to the skillet with the tuna. Add the tomatoes and arugula, then toss well. Serve hot.

ORECCHIETTE WITH STRACCIATELLA CHEESE

SERVES: 2
PREP: 5 MINS
COOK: 15 MINS

This recipe is one of my quick pasta dishes. Simple, but full of flavor, the stracciatella cheese will complete the dish with its unique creaminess and its fresh and delicate taste.

INGREDIENTS

6 ounces (180g) dried orecchiette

2 tablespoons extra-virgin olive oil

1 garlic clove, lightly crushed

1 cup (250g) strained pureed tomatoes (passata)

3½ ounces (100g) stracciatella cheese

few basil leaves

salt and pepper

1. Bring a large saucepan of water to a boil, add salt, then add the pasta and cook for 2 minutes less than the package directions.

2. Meanwhile, heat the oil in a skillet over medium heat, add the garlic, and cook until fragrant. Add the strained pureed tomatoes, season to taste, and cook for 10 minutes, adding a little water if necessary. Remove and discard the garlic.

3. Drain the pasta, setting aside 2 tablespoons of the cooking water. Add the pasta to the strained pureed tomatoes, and mix and toss until everything is combined, adding the reserved cooking water, if necessary.

4. Divide the pasta among serving plates, dot with the stracciatella and basil, and serve.

PACCHERI WITH MIXED TOMATOES

SERVES: 2 + LEFTOVERS
PREP: 5 MINS
COOK: 25 MINS

INGREDIENTS

2¼ pounds (1kg) ripe tomatoes, such as cherry, plum, or Roma

6 tablespoons extra-virgin olive oil

1 garlic clove, lightly crushed

1 basil sprig

6 ounces (180g) dried paccheri

salt and pepper

grated Parmesan cheese, for serving

This recipe highlights one of the most important stars of Italian cuisine—the tomato. This quantity of sauce will be more than you need for the recipe, and the remainder can be frozen for up to six months.

1. Preheat the oven to 350°F (180°C).

2. Place the tomatoes on a baking sheet, add 4 tablespoons of the oil, the garlic, and the basil sprig, and season with salt and pepper. Bake in the oven for about 25 minutes. When ready, remove and discard the garlic and blend most of the tomatoes in a blender, setting aside a few for garnishing.

3. Meanwhile, bring a large pan of water to a boil, add salt, then add the pasta and cook for 1 minute less than the package directions.

4. When the pasta is cooked, drain and return to the pan. Add the tomato sauce and the remaining oil, and mix well to combine. Garnish with the reserved tomatoes and serve hot with grated Parmesan.

PAPPARDELLE WITH SMOKED SALMON

SERVES: 2
PREP: 5 MINS
COOK: 10 MINS

INGREDIENTS

2 tablespoons extra-virgin olive oil

½ onion, finely chopped

scant ½ cup (100ml) half and half (single cream)

⅓ pound (150g) dried pappardelle

⅓ pound (150g) smoked salmon, cut into short strips

salt and pepper

chopped parsley leaves, for serving

Quick and easy to prepare, cream is the key ingredient in this recipe as it tones down the strong taste of the smoked salmon and adds a richness to the dish.

1. Heat the oil in a large skillet over low to medium heat, add the onion, and sauté for 3 minutes. Add the half and half, season, and cook for 3 minutes.

2. Meanwhile, bring a large saucepan of water to a boil, add salt, then add the pasta and cook for 2 minutes less than the package directions. Drain the pasta, setting aside 1 ladleful of the cooking water, and add to the sauce. Stir and toss to combine, adding a splash of the pasta cooking water, if necessary.

3. Add the salmon to the sauce and mix again. Serve with a sprinkling of parsley.

CASARECCE WITH ROASTED PEPPERS

SERVES: 2

PREP: 5 MINS

COOK: 20 MINS

If you can, use ripe San Marzano tomatoes in this dish as they are sweeter and have thicker flesh and fewer seeds than other varieties.

INGREDIENTS

6 tablespoons extra-virgin olive oil

½ onion, thinly sliced

1½ cups (250g) coarsely chopped ripe tomatoes

2 red bell peppers, halved and seeded

6 ounces (180g) dried casarecce

salt and pepper

basil leaves, for serving

1. Preheat the oven to 400°F (200°C).

2. Heat 4 tablespoons of the oil in a saucepan, add the onion, and sauté for 5 minutes. Add the tomatoes and cook for 15 minutes.

3. Meanwhile, place the pepper, cut-side up, in a roasting dish and drizzle with the remaining oil. Season with salt and pepper and bake in the oven for 15 to 20 minutes. When ready, remove the skin, cut the flesh into strips, then add to the tomatoes and mix well.

4. At the same time, bring a large pan of water to a boil, add salt, then add the pasta and cook for 2 minutes less than the package directions.

5. Drain the pasta, setting aside 2 tablespoons of the cooking water. Add the pasta to the sauce and toss, adding a little of the reserved cooking water, if necessary, until it is well combined. Serve with basil.

SPAGHETTI ALLA NERANO

SERVES : 2
PREP : 5 MINS
COOK : 15 MINS

INGREDIENTS

1 cup (250ml) sunflower oil

3 medium zucchini, sliced into thin circles

6 ounces (180g) dried spaghetti

2 tablespoons butter

1 cup (100g) grated provolone del Monaco or other semihard cow's milk cheese

salt and pepper

torn basil leaves torn, for serving (optional)

Created in 1952 by a woman called Maria Grazia from the village of Nerano, this recipe has been passed down by generations. Her restaurant is still the best place to eat this dish, but my recipe here will do if you can't get to Nerano.

1. Line a baking sheet with paper towels. Heat the oil in a large skillet over medium to high heat and fry the zucchini slices in batches until golden brown. Drain on the lined baking sheet. Season with salt and keep warm.

2. Meanwhile, bring a large saucepan of water to a boil, add salt, then add the pasta and cook for 2 minutes less than the package directions.

3. Drain the pasta, setting aside a ladleful of the cooking water. Return the pasta to the pan and add the zucchini, butter, and half of the grated cheese. Start to mix and toss, adding the reserved cooking water, a little at a time, with the remaining cheese, to create a silky and creamy sauce that coats the spaghetti. Serve with torn basil leaves (if using) and pepper.

UNDER 20 MINUTES

SPAGHETTI WITH CAPERS AND OLIVES

SERVES: 2
PREP: 5 MINS
COOK: 12 MINS

A tasty, vibrant, and classic tomato sauce, this is ideal for a simple and budget-friendly midweek dinner.

INGREDIENTS

6 ounces (180g) dried spaghetti

1 tablespoon extra-virgin olive oil

1 garlic clove, lightly crushed

½ chile, seeded and finely chopped

2 tablespoons salted capers, rinsed and coarsely chopped

12 black olives, pitted and halved

1 (15-ounce / 425g) can peeled tomatoes, lightly crushed

chopped parsley, for sprinkling

salt and pepper

1. Bring a large pan of water to a boil, add salt, then add the pasta and cook for 2 minutes less than the package directions.

2. Meanwhile, heat the oil in a large skillet over medium heat, add the garlic and chile, and fry for 2 minutes. Add the capers, olives, and tomatoes, mix well, and cook for 8 minutes. Season to taste. Remove and discard the garlic.

3. Drain the pasta, setting aside 2 tablespoons of the cooking water. Add the pasta to the skillet with the sauce and toss until the pasta is fully coated, adding a splash of the reserved cooking water, if necessary. Sprinkle with parsley and serve.

ASPARAGUS CARBONARA

SERVES: 2

PREP: 5 MINS

COOK: 10 MINS

INGREDIENTS

1 bunch of asparagus, woody stalks removed

3 tablespoons extra-virgin olive oil

6 ounces (180g) dried tortiglioni

3 egg yolks

3 tablespoons grated Parmesan cheese, plus extra for serving

salt and pepper

This is an alternative to the classic carbonara recipe where, instead of guanciale, asparagus is used. Light and fresh, this is a perfect dish to prepare in spring and early summer when asparagus is in season.

1. Keeping the asparagus tips intact, cut the asparagus stems into ½-inch (1cm) circles. Heat the oil in a large skillet, add the asparagus, and fry for 2 minutes. Season with salt and pepper, add 1 ladleful of boiling water, and cook for another 5 minutes. Transfer to a large bowl.

2. Meanwhile, bring a large saucepan of water to a boil, add salt, then add the pasta and cook for 2 minutes less than the package directions.

3. Mix the egg yolks, Parmesan, and a splash of the pasta cooking water together in a small bowl until creamy.

4. Drain the pasta, setting aside 2 tablespoons of the cooking water. Add the pasta to the asparagus together with the egg mixture and toss to combine, adding a splash of the reserved cooking water, if necessary. Season with pepper, sprinkle with Parmesan, and serve.

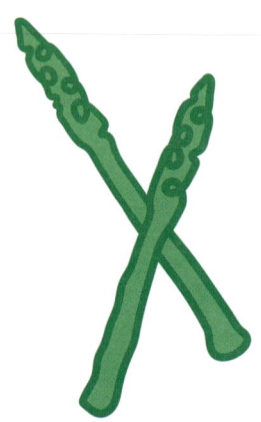

CRAB LINGUINE

SERVES: 2

PREP: 5 MINS

COOK: 10 MINS

INGREDIENTS

6 ounces (180g) dried linguine

2 tablespoons extra-virgin olive oil

1 garlic clove, lightly crushed

½ chile, seeded and chopped

10 cherry tomatoes, halved

⅓ pound (150g) fresh white crabmeat

chopped parsley, for sprinkling

1 tablespoon lemon juice

salt and pepper

Crabmeat has a delicate flavor suitable for making many recipes like this quick linguine. A tasty dish, perfect for a summer evening.

1. Bring a large saucepan of water to a boil, add salt, then add the pasta and cook for 2 minutes less than the package directions.

2. Meanwhile, heat the oil in a large skillet over medium heat, add the garlic and chile, and fry for 2 minutes. Add the tomatoes and crabmeat and cook over low heat for a few minutes.

3. Drain the pasta, setting aside 2 tablespoons of the cooking water. Add the pasta to the skillet and toss together for 1 minute, or until the pasta is fully coated. Season to taste, then sprinkle with parsley and finish with the lemon juice.

AMATRICIANA

SERVES: 2
PREP: 5 MINS
COOK: 15 MINS

INGREDIENTS

6 ounces (180g) dried
spaghetti

2¼ ounces (65g)
guanciale, rind removed
and cut into small batons

½ chile, seeded
and finely chopped

2 tablespoons white wine

1 (15-ounce / 425g)
can peeled tomatoes,
lightly crushed

grated Pecorino Romano
cheese, for sprinkling

salt and pepper

Created in a town called Amatrice, just
62 miles from Rome, this is a simple yet
delicious dish. You can use fresh tomatoes
when in season.

1. Bring a large saucepan of water to a boil, add salt,
then add the pasta and cook for 2 minutes less than the
package directions.

2. Add the guanciale and chile to a large nonstick skillet
and cook over medium to high heat for 5 minutes, stirring
continuously. Add the wine and stir to remove any stuck-
on bits on the bottom of the pan. Add the tomatoes. Bring
just to a boil, then simmer for 5 minutes, or until it starts
to thicken. Season to taste.

3. Drain the pasta, setting aside 1 ladleful of the cooking
water. Add the pasta to the pan with the sauce and
toss until the pasta is fully coated, adding a splash of
the reserved cooking water, if necessary. Sprinkle with
pecorino cheese and serve immediately.

FUSILLI WITH TOMATO SAUCE AND RICOTTA

SERVES: 2

PREP: 5 MINS

COOK: 15 MINS

A very quick and tasty dish that takes minutes to prepare. Try to use a good-quality fresh ricotta for a great result.

INGREDIENTS

6 ounces (180g) dried fusilli

2 tablespoons extra-virgin olive oil

1 garlic clove, lightly crushed

1 ¼ cups (300ml) strained pureed tomatoes (passata)

few basil leaves

1 cup (200g) fresh ricotta cheese

salt and pepper

grated Parmesan cheese, for sprinkling

1. Bring a large saucepan of water to a boil, add salt, then add the pasta and cook for 2 minutes less than the package directions.

2. Heat the oil in another pan, add the garlic, and fry for a few minutes, being careful that it doesn't burn. Add the strained pureed tomatoes, season to taste, and cook over medium to high heat for 8 minutes, stirring constantly. Add the basil and remove the garlic.

3. Meanwhile, using a fork, whisk the ricotta in a medium bowl, then add the tomato sauce and mix to combine.

4. Drain the pasta, setting aside 2 tablespoons of the cooking water. Add the pasta to the bowl with the ricotta and tomato, then toss and mix the pasta until it is fully coated, adding a splash of the reserved cooking water, if necessary. Serve hot with grated Parmesan.

PAPPARDELLE WITH MUSHROOMS

SERVES: 2
PREP: 5 MINS
COOK: 10 MINS

INGREDIENTS

1 cup (20g)
dried porcini

6 ounces (180g)
dried egg pappardelle

2 tablespoons
extra-virgin olive oil

3 tablespoons butter

1 garlic clove, minced

⅓ pound (150g) mixed
mushrooms, cleaned and
sliced

1 sage sprig

salt and pepper

grated Parmesan cheese,
for serving

The secret to this dish is using a variety of fresh mushrooms with the dried porcini to take weeknight cooking to a whole new level.

1. Soak the porcini in a bowl of water for 15 minutes, then drain and squeeze out to remove any excess water.

2. Meanwhile, bring a large saucepan of water to a boil, add salt, then add the pasta and cook for 2 minutes less than the package directions.

3. Heat the oil and butter in a large skillet over low heat, add the garlic, and fry for 1 minute. Add the mushrooms, including the porcini, and sage, and sauté for a few minutes until they are cooked through. Season to taste.

4. Drain the pasta, setting aside 2 tablespoons of the pasta cooking water. Add the pasta to the skillet with the mushrooms and toss until the pasta is fully coated, adding a splash of the reserved cooking water, if necessary. Serve with grated Parmesan.

TROFIE WITH GORGONZOLA, THYME, AND WALNUTS

SERVES : 2
PREP : 5 MINS
COOK : 10 MINS

INGREDIENTS

6 ounces (180g) trofie

¼ cup (60ml) half and half (single cream)

⅓ pound (150g) sweet Gorgonzola, cubed

½ cup (50g) chopped walnuts

few thyme sprigs

salt and pepper

This is an irresistible classic combo: Gorgonzola and walnuts. In Italy there are two types of Gorgonzola—sweet, and spicy. I used the sweet one in this dish as it is soft, buttery, and creamy. It is also easier to melt than the spicy one, which is crumblier and firmer. If you can't find the sweet, soft version, then any other will do.

1. Bring a large saucepan of water to a boil, add salt, then add the pasta and cook for 1 minute less than the package directions.

2. Warm the cream in a pan over low heat. Add the Gorgonzola and season to taste. Cook for a few minutes until the cheese is completely melted.

3. Drain the pasta, setting aside 1 tablespoon of the cooking water. Add the pasta to the pan and gently toss until everything is combined, adding the reserved cooking water, if necessary. Sprinkle the chopped walnuts over the top and serve with pepper and thyme.

TAGLIATELLE WITH ZUCCHINI FLOWERS

SERVES: 2

PREP: 5 MINS

COOK: 10 MINS

INGREDIENTS

6 ounces (180g) dried egg tagliatelle

3 tablespoons butter

1 garlic clove, lightly crushed

2 small zucchini, julienned

6 zucchini flowers, stalks detached and pistils removed

2 to 3 pinches of saffron threads

grated Parmesan cheese, for sprinkling

salt and pepper

Zucchini flowers aren't just for stuffing. In this recipe they are added to the zucchini, where they wilt just like tender greens.

1. Bring a large saucepan of water to a boil, add salt, then add the pasta and cook for 1 minute less than the package directions.

2. Meanwhile, heat half of the butter, the garlic, zucchini, and 1 cup (250ml) water in a large skillet and cook for 7 minutes. Add the zucchini flowers and saffron and cook for another 1 minute.

3. Drain the pasta, setting aside ½ cup (120ml) of the cooking water. Add the pasta to the pan with the remaining butter and the grated Parmesan and toss the pasta, adding a splash of the reserved cooking water, if necessary, for 1 minute. Season to taste and serve.

CASARECCE WITH PESTO AND VEGETABLES

SERVES: 2

PREP: 5 MINS

COOK: 10 MINS

This is a very simple, light, and tasty summer dish that can also be enjoyed cold.

INGREDIENTS

6 ounces (180g) dried casarecce

2 tablespoons extra-virgin olive oil

1 zucchini, diced

1 small eggplant, diced

⅓ pound (150g) mixed ripe tomatoes, cut into quarters

1 quantity of Classic Pesto (page 95)

salt and pepper

grated Parmesan cheese, for serving

1. Bring a large saucepan of water to a boil, add salt, then add the pasta and cook for 2 minutes less than the package directions.

2. Meanwhile, heat the oil in a large skillet, add the zucchini and eggplant, and stir-fry for 5 minutes. Add the tomatoes and 1 ladleful of boiling water and cook for another 5 minutes. Season with salt and pepper.

3. Combine the pesto with the vegetables in a large bowl. Drain the pasta, add it to the vegetables, toss to combine, and serve with grated Parmesan.

TONNARELLI WITH CRISPY PANCETTA AND ASPARAGUS

SERVES: 2

PREP: 5 MINS

COOK: 15 MINS

This dish combines the delicacy of asparagus with the strong character of pancetta and Pecorino Romano cheese—three flavors that mix perfectly in this easy recipe.

INGREDIENTS

¼ cup (60ml) extra-virgin olive oil

¼ onion, finely chopped

9 ounces (250g) asparagus, trimmed, stems cut into circles, and tips cut lengthwise

⅓ pound (150g) dried tonnarelli

1¾ ounces (50g) pancetta, diced

grated Parmesan cheese, for sprinkling

salt and pepper

1. Heat the oil in a skillet, add the onion, and sauté for 2 minutes. Add the asparagus stems, 1 ladleful of boiling water, and season to taste. Cook for 5 minutes. Add the asparagus tips and cook for another 5 minutes. Remove from the skillet and set aside.

2. Meanwhile, bring a large saucepan of water to a boil, add salt, then add the pasta and cook for 2 minutes less than the package directions.

3. Return the skillet to the heat, add the pancetta, and fry for 3 minutes, or until crispy.

4. Drain the pasta, setting aside 2 tablespoons of the cooking water. Add the pasta to the pan with the pancetta, then add the asparagus and toss until the pasta is fully coated, adding a splash of the reserved cooking water, if necessary. Serve with Parmesan.

TAGLIOLINI WITH SHRIMP AND LEMON

SERVES: 2
PREP: 5 MINS
COOK: 10 MINS

INGREDIENTS

6 ounces (180g)
fresh tagliolini

2 tablespoons extra-virgin
olive oil

1 garlic clove, lightly
crushed

7 ounces (200g)
small shrimp, peeled

¼ cup (60ml) white wine

grated zest of ½ lemon

chopped parsley, for
sprinkling

salt and pepper

This seafood pasta is very easy and can be prepared in just a few minutes. It has a real explosion of taste and aroma, as the acidic note of the lemon goes very well with the sweetness of the shrimp.

1. Bring a large saucepan of water to a boil, add salt, then add the pasta and cook for 2 minutes less than the package directions.

2. Meanwhile, heat the oil in a large skillet over medium to high heat, add the garlic, and fry for 2 minutes. Add the shrimp and cook for 1 minute. Add the wine and let bubble for 2 minutes. Season to taste. Remove and discard the garlic.

3. Drain the pasta, setting aside 1 tablespoon of the cooking water. Add the pasta to the pan with the shrimp and toss until the pasta is coated, adding a splash of the reserved cooking water, if necessary. Remove from the heat, stir through the lemon zest and parsley, and serve.

PACCHERI WITH TOMATOES AND MOZZARELLA

SERVES: 2
PREP: 5 MINS
COOK: 15 MINS

Paccheri is a pasta from Campania. With its unique tubular shape, it has the ability to capture and soak up sauces perfectly.

INGREDIENTS

6 ounces (180g) dried paccheri

2 tablespoons extra-virgin olive oil

1 garlic clove, lightly crushed

1¾ cups (300g) mixed cherry tomatoes

1 basil sprig, leaves picked

1 small mozzarella ball, diced

salt and pepper

1. Bring a large saucepan of water to a boil, add salt, then add the pasta and cook for 2 minutes less than the package directions.

2. Meanwhile, heat the oil in a skillet over low to medium heat, add the garlic, and cook for 5 minutes, stirring continuously. Add the tomatoes and basil, season to taste, and cook for 10 minutes, or until the tomatoes have burst. Remove and discard the garlic.

3. Drain the pasta, setting aside 2 tablespoons of the cooking water. Add the pasta to the skillet with the tomatoes and sprinkle over the mozzarella. Increase the heat and cook, stirring, until the mozzarella melts and the pasta is fully coated in the sauce, adding a splash of the reserved cooking water, if necessary. Serve immediately.

CARBONARA

SERVES: 2

PREP: 5 MINS

COOK: 10 MINS

INGREDIENTS

6 ounces (180g) dried spaghetti

2¾ ounces (80g) guanciale, rind removed and cut into small batons

3 medium egg yolks

2 tablespoons grated Pecorino Romano cheese

salt and pepper

This is one of the most copied and reinvented dishes of Italian cuisine, and since 2017, there has even been a National Carbonara day to celebrate this dish. Pasta lovers everywhere identify this dish as the taste of Italy.

1. Bring a large saucepan of water to a boil, add salt, then add the pasta and cook for 2 minutes less than the package directions.

2. Cook the guanciale in a large nonstick skillet over medium to high heat for 5 minutes, stirring continuously, until it is just golden. Turn off the heat.

3. Meanwhile, whisk the egg yolks, cheese, and salt and pepper together in a medium bowl. Add 1 tablespoon of the pasta cooking water to loosen up the mixture.

4. Drain the pasta, setting aside 1 ladleful of the cooking water. Add the pasta to the pan with the guanciale. Return to the heat, add a splash of the reserved cooking water, and sauté for a minute. Remove from the heat and pour the egg mixture into the pan. Toss the pasta until it is fully coated, adding another splash of the reserved water, if necessary. Serve immediately.

UNDER 20 MINUTES

BUTTER AND SAGE RAVIOLI

SERVES: 2
PREP: 5 MINS
COOK: 10 MINS

INGREDIENTS

4 tablespoons butter

6 sage leaves

6 ounces (180g)
fresh ravioli

grated Parmesan cheese,
for sprinkling

salt and pepper

A classic of Italian cuisine, stuffed pasta such as ravioli sometimes just needs a delicate and light sauce. This sauce can also be used with fresh or store-bought gnocchi. I used spinach and ricotta ravioli, but there are lots of different fillings available, so use your favorite ravioli, if you prefer.

1. Melt the butter in a large skillet, and when it starts to get a good sizzle, add the sage leaves. Continue cooking, swirling the pan for 5 minutes, or until the sage is crisp and the butter turns brown in color. Season to taste.

2. Meanwhile, bring a large saucepan of water to a boil, add salt, then add the ravioli and cook for 1 minute less than the package directions.

3. Drain the ravioli, add them to the skillet, and gently toss until combined with the butter and sage. Sprinkle over the grated Parmesan and serve.

FOUR CHEESE PENNE

SERVES: 2
PREP: 5 MINS
COOK: 10 MINS

INGREDIENTS

6 ounces (180g)
dried penne

6 tablespoons whole milk

2 tablespoons grated
Parmesan cheese

1 ounce (30g)
sweet Gorgonzola, cubed

½ ounce (15g)
Fontina cheese, cubed

1 ounce (30g) Taleggio
cheese, cubed

salt and pepper

The perfect dish for cheese lovers, this recipe has a rich and substantial sauce, as it's made with four different types of cheese. You can personalize the cheeses according to your own taste.

1. Bring a large saucepan of water to a boil, add salt, then add the pasta and cook for 1 minute less than the package directions.

2. Meanwhile, warm the milk in a large skillet and add all the cheeses. Cook over low heat, stirring for 5 minutes, or until the cheeses melt into the milk.

3. Drain the pasta, setting aside 1 tablespoon of the cooking water. Add the pasta to the skillet and gently toss until combined and thickened, adding a splash of the reserved cooking water, if necessary. Season to taste and serve.

SWEET PEA GNOCCHI

SERVES: 2

PREP: 5 MINS

COOK: 10 MINS

A perfect spring recipe where the vibrant green color of peas has no rival. Use store-bought gnocchi and fresh or frozen peas.

INGREDIENTS

2 tablespoons extra-virgin olive oil, plus extra for drizzling

1 tablespoon soffritto (page 10)

1 ¼ cups (150g) fresh or frozen peas

2 handfuls of pea shoots

6 ounces (180g) store-bought gnocchi

salt and pepper

grated zest of ½ lemon, for serving

Parmesan cheese shavings, for serving

1. Heat the oil in a skillet over medium heat, add the soffritto, and sauté for a few minutes. Add the peas and cook for 5 minutes. Blitz half of the peas with a handful of the pea shoots in a blender or food processor until smooth. Season to taste and set aside.

2. Meanwhile, bring a large saucepan of water to a boil. Add salt, then add the gnocchi and cook according to the package directions, or until they float to the top. Drain, setting aside a ladleful of the cooking water, and add them to the peas in the skillet. Mix to combine, adding a little of the cooking water, if necessary.

3. Spoon the reserved pea puree into serving bowls, add the gnocchi, drizzle with oil, and serve with pepper, grated lemon zest, Parmesan shavings, and the remaining pea shoots.

CLASSIC PESTO

SUNDRIED TOMATO PESTO

OLIVE PESTO

TUSCAN KALE AND ALMOND PESTO

PESTO FOUR WAYS

CLASSIC PESTO

MAKES: 1 CUP (250ML)
PREP: 15 MINS
COOK: 2 MINS

INGREDIENTS

⅓ cup (50g) pine nuts

2¾ ounces (80g) basil

1¾ ounces (50g)
Parmesan cheese

⅔ cup (150ml) olive oil

2 garlic cloves

salt and pepper

Pesto can elevate an ordinary pasta dish into something special. There are so many varieties to choose from, but I have included my top four favorites here.

1. Heat a small skillet over low heat. Add the pine nuts and fry until golden, shaking the pan occasionally.

2. Transfer the pine nuts to a food processor with the basil, Parmesan, olive oil, and garlic and whizz until smooth. Season to taste. Serve or transfer to a small airtight jar and store in the refrigerator for up to three days.

TUSCAN KALE AND ALMOND PESTO
Follow the recipe above, but use 30 toasted almonds instead of the pine nuts and add 2½ cups (250g) finely shredded Tuscan kale to the food processor.

OLIVE PESTO
Follow the recipe above, adding 2½ cups (250g) pitted black olives to the food processor.

SUNDRIED TOMATO PESTO
Follow the recipe above adding 2½ cups (280g) chopped sundried tomatoes, 2 tablespoons blanched almonds, ½ cup (10g) basil, and olive oil, if needed.

BUCATINI WITH KALE PESTO

SERVES: 2
PREP: 5 MINS
COOK: 10 MINS

INGREDIENTS

6 ounces (180g) dried bucatini

2 tablespoons extra-virgin olive oil

1¾ ounces (50g) pancetta, cubed

½ quantity of Tuscan Kale and Almond Pesto (page 95)

grated Pecorino Romano cheese, for sprinkling

1 burrata, halved

salt and pepper

Normally Tuscan kale is an ingredient to use in the winter, such as in ribollita, but here it is perfect for this easy-to-make pasta. It is a dish full of goodness from the iron-rich kale.

1. Bring a large saucepan of water to a boil, add salt, then add the pasta and cook for 1 minute less than the package directions.

2. Meanwhile, heat the oil in a large skillet, add the pancetta, and cook for a few minutes, stirring frequently. When crunchy, remove the pancetta with a slotted spoon and set aside.

3. Place the pesto into a large bowl and loosen up with 2 tablespoons of the pasta cooking water. Drain the pasta, setting aside 2 tablespoons of the cooking water. Add the pasta to the pesto and mix until combined, adding little of the reserved cooking water, if necessary. Add the pancetta, pecorino, and burrata and serve.

UNDER 20 MINUTES

FUSILLI WITH RADICCHIO AND GORGONZOLA

SERVES: 2
PREP: 5 MINS
COOK: 10 MINS

Radicchio and Gorgonzola are a classic combination, so this dish is dedicated to the most daring of palates.

INGREDIENTS

6 ounces (180g) dried fusilli

1 tablespoon extra-virgin olive oil

3 ½ ounces (100g) speck, cubed

1 small head of radicchio, sliced

3 ½ ounces (100g) sweet Gorgonzola cheese, cubed

grated Parmesan cheese, for sprinkling

salt and pepper

1. Bring a large saucepan of water to a boil, add salt, then add the pasta and cook for 1 minute less than the package directions.

2. Meanwhile, heat the oil in a large skillet, add the speck, and cook for a few minutes, stirring frequently. When crunchy, remove the speck with a slotted spoon and set aside.

3. Add the radicchio and 2 tablespoons of the pasta cooking water to the skillet and simmer for 1 minute. Add the Gorgonzola and stir until it is completely melted.

4. Drain the pasta, setting aside 1 tablespoon of the cooking water. Add the pasta to the skillet and gently toss until it is combined, adding a splash of the reserved cooking water, if necessary. Season to taste and serve with the reserved speck and grated Parmesan.

PASTA ALLA GRICIA

SERVES: 2

PREP: 5 MINS

COOK: 10 MINS

INGREDIENTS

6 ounces (180g) dried
rigatoni

4½ ounces (130g)
guanciale, rind removed
and cut into small batons

5 tablespoons grated
Pecorino Romano cheese

salt and pepper

One of the most iconic dishes in Roman
cuisine, it is also known as "white
Amatriciana," as there are no tomatoes.
It relies for its deliciousness on a sauce made
with guanciale ("cured pork jowl") instead.

1. Bring a large saucepan of water to a boil, add salt,
then add the pasta and cook for 2 minutes less than
the package instructions.

2. Cook the guanciale in a large skillet over medium to
high heat for 5 minutes, stirring continuously, until it is just
golden. Remove and set aside, leaving all the cooking
juices in the pan.

3. Pour a ladleful of the cooking water into the skillet and
stir to make an emulsion. Drain the pasta, setting aside
2 tablespoons of the cooking water. Add the pasta to the
skillet and cook, tossing and stirring, for 1 minute. Remove
from the heat, add the cheese, and toss until the pasta
is fully coated in the cheese, adding a splash of the
reserved cooking water, if necessary. Add the guanciale
and season with pepper before serving.

CALAMARATA

SERVES: 2
PREP: 5 MINS
COOK: 15 MINS

INGREDIENTS

2 tablespoons extra-virgin olive oil

½ chile, finely chopped

1 garlic clove, lightly crushed

7 ounces (200g) squid, cleaned and cut into rings

2 tablespoons white wine

7 ounces (200g) vine tomatoes, halved

6 ounces (180g) dried calamarata

salt

chopped parsley, for garnishing

This is a very simple, easy, and quick-to-prepare fish dish. The combination of squid and this shape of pasta that resembles squid rings, from which it takes its name, is perfect.

1. Heat the oil in a large saucepan, add the chile and garlic, and fry until fragrant. Add the squid and cook for a few minutes. Add the wine and once the alcohol has evaporated, add the tomatoes and simmer for 10 minutes. Remove and discard the garlic.

2. Meanwhile, bring a large saucepan of water to a boil, add salt, then add the pasta and cook for 2 minutes less than the package directions.

3. Drain the pasta, setting aside 2 tablespoons of the cooking water. Add the pasta to the squid mixture and toss until well combined, adding the reserved cooking water, if necessary. Garnish with parsley and serve.

ORIGINAL FETTUCCINE ALFREDO

SERVES:2

PREP:5 MINS

COOK:10 MINS

INGREDIENTS

6 ounces (180g) dried egg fettuccine

4 tablespoons butter

4 tablespoons grated Parmesan cheese

salt and pepper

This recipe is a Roman dish: pasta is tossed in a creamy emulsion of just Parmesan and butter to create a flavorful sauce. Do not mistake it for the American version, which uses cream, garlic, butter, and cheese.

1. Bring a large saucepan of water to a boil, add salt, then add the pasta and cook for 2 minutes less than the package directions.

2. Meanwhile, melt half of the butter with 1 tablespoon of the pasta cooking water in a large skillet.

3. Drain the pasta, setting aside ½ cup (120ml) of the cooking water. Add the pasta to the skillet over low to medium heat, then add the remaining butter, salt, and a few tablespoons of the reserved cooking water. Cook the pasta for 1 minute, adding more of the cooking water, if necessary. Turn off the heat, season with pepper, add the Parmesan, and toss to combine. Serve immediately.

SUNDRIED TOMATO SPAGHETTI WITH CAPERS

SERVES: 2
PREP: 5 MINS
COOK: 10 MINS

This quick and easy pantry vegetarian recipe, with its tangy and subtly sweet flavor, evokes the seductive scents and flavors of Sicily.

INGREDIENTS

6 ounces (180g) dried spaghetti

2 tablespoons extra-virgin olive oil

1 tablespoon capers, rinsed

1 garlic clove, lightly crushed

½ chile, finely diced

½ cup (60g) sundried tomatoes, drained and coarsely chopped

salt and pepper

chopped parsley, for garnishing

1. Bring a large saucepan of water to a boil, add salt, then add the pasta and cook for 2 minutes less than the package directions.

2. Meanwhile, heat the oil in a large skillet over medium heat, add the capers, and cook for a few minutes until they are puffed and starting to brown. Remove from the pan and set aside.

3. Add the garlic, chile, and tomatoes to the skillet and fry for 3 minutes. Remove and discard the garlic.

4. Drain the pasta, setting aside 1 ladleful of the cooking water. Add the pasta to the skillet and toss to combine, adding the reserved cooking water. Season to taste.

5. Serve the pasta with the chopped parsley and fried capers sprinkled on top.

QUICK AND EASY
ONE POT

BROKEN PASTA WITH CHICKPEAS

SERVES: 2
PREP: 5 MINS
COOK: 15 MINS

INGREDIENTS

2 tablespoons extra-virgin olive oil

1 garlic clove, slightly crushed

1 rosemary sprig

1 (15-ounce / 425g) can chickpeas, washed and drained

6 ounces (180g) broken dried mafaldine

grated Parmesan cheese, for sprinkling

salt and pepper

Delicious, comforting, and healthy, this is one of my favorite winter "pasta soups." Pasta and chickpeas are both staples in Italian cuisine and canned chickpeas work well here, saving hours of cooking time.

1. Heat the oil in a pan, add the garlic, and fry for a few minutes, being careful that it doesn't burn. Add the rosemary and fry for a few seconds. Add the chickpeas and let them brown for a few minutes. Pour in 2½ cups (600ml) boiling water, stir, and cook for 5 minutes. Remove and discard the garlic and rosemary.

2. Let cool slightly, then blend half of the soup in a blender until smooth. Return it to the pan. Add the pasta to the pan and cook until it is al dente, adding more water if necessary. Season to taste, then sprinkle with grated Parmesan before serving.

TROFIE WITH PESTO GENOVESE

SERVES: 2
PREP: 5 MINS
COOK: 15 MINS

INGREDIENTS

6 ounces (180g)
dried trofie

2¾ ounces (80g) potatoes,
peeled and diced

2¾ ounces (80g) green
beans, trimmed and cut in
3 pieces

½ quantity of Classic Pesto
(page 94)

grated Parmesan cheese,
for sprinkling

salt and pepper

This is a traditional pasta recipe from the
region of Liguria in Italy. Potatoes and green
beans are common additions, making this
a perfect complete and balanced dish.

1. Fill a saucepan a third of the way with water, then
bring to a boil, add salt, then add the trofie and potatoes.
After 6 minutes, add the green beans and cook for 1
minute less than the package directions.

2. Meanwhile, place the pesto in a large bowl and
add 2 tablespoons of the pasta cooking water. Drain
the pasta, potatoes, and green beans, setting aside 2
tablespoons of the cooking water, and add them to the
pesto. Mix until combined, adding a little of the cooking
water, if necessary. Sprinkle with Parmesan and serve.

CONCHIGLIE WITH LENTILS

SERVES: 2
PREP: 5 MINS
COOK: 35 MINS

INGREDIENTS

2 tablespoons extra-virgin olive oil

2 garlic cloves, lightly crushed

10½ ounces (300g) soffritto (page 10)

1 tablespoon strained pureed tomatoes (passata)

1 bouquet garni with thyme and parsley

¾ cup (150g) dried Castelluccio or Puy lentils, washed

4½ ounces (120g) dried conchiglie

salt and pepper

A Neapolitan staple, this is one of the best examples of how to turn a few basic ingredients into something special. For this recipe, I used Castelluccio lentils from Norcia, which are small, brown lentils with a nutty and earthy flavor.

I. Combine all the ingredients in a large saucepan and add 1¾ cups (400ml) water. Bring to a boil over high heat and cook, stirring and turning the pasta until it is al dente, the lentils are cooked, and the water is completely evaporated. Season with salt and pepper and serve.

MINESTRONE WITH ORZO PASTA

SERVES: 2 + LEFTOVERS
PREP: 5 MINS
COOK: 25 MINS

INGREDIENTS

2 tablespoons extra-virgin olive oil, plus extra for drizzling

10½ ounces (300g) soffritto (page 10)

4 large potatoes, cut into cubes

½ small pumpkin, peeled, seeded, and cut into cubes

1¾ ounces (50g) mixed ripe tomatoes

7 ounces (200g) mixed seasonal vegetables, sliced (see note)

3½ ounces (100g) dried orzo

grated Parmesan cheese, for sprinkling

salt and pepper

There are different versions of minestrone in Italy, but in general, it is made with seasonal vegetables, including ingredients like potatoes, squashes, or pulses to thicken the soup, plus pasta, rice, or grains. To enhance the flavor of this recipe, you can add a Parmesan rind, but just remember to remove whatever is left of the rind before serving. Depending on the season you can use zucchini, bell peppers, spinach, peas, green beans, or cauliflower, broccoli, Swiss chard, and Tuscan kale.

1. Heat the oil in a large saucepan, add the soffritto, and sauté for a few minutes. Add the potatoes and pumpkin, stir, and cook for 5 minutes. Add the tomatoes and the remaining vegetables and cook, stirring, for 1 minute before pouring in enough boiling water to cover all the vegetables.

2. Cook for 10 minutes, or until the potatoes and pumpkin are tender. Add the pasta and more boiling water, if necessary and cook for 1 minute less than the package directions. Season, sprinkle with grated Parmesan, and drizzle with oil before serving.

SPAGHETTI WITH GARLIC, OIL, AND CHILE

SPAGHETTI WITH BREADCRUMBS

SPAGHETTI WITH LEMON

SPAGHETTI WITH ANCHOVIES

SPAGHETTI FOUR WAYS

GARLIC, OIL, AND CHILE

SERVES: 2
PREP: 5 MINS
COOK: 10 MINS

These are the quintessential dinner-saving recipes, widely popular for being inexpensive, quick, and simple to prepare.

INGREDIENTS

3 tablespoons extra-virgin olive oil

1 garlic clove, diced

1 red chile, thinly sliced

6 ounces (180g) cooked spaghetti

2 parsley sprigs, finely chopped (optional)

1. Heat the oil in a large pan, add the garlic, and fry for 2 minutes. Add the chile and fry for a few seconds.

2. When draining the cooked spaghetti, set aside 2 tablespoons of the cooking water. Add the pasta to the pan with the cooking water and toss to coat in the oil and garlic. Sprinkle with parsley (if using) before serving.

BREADCRUMBS

Fry 1 crushed garlic clove and 2 tablespoons toasted breadcrumbs in 2 tablespoons oil for 2 minutes. Add the pasta, reserved water, and toss. Season with pepper.

LEMON

Heat 1 tablespoon olive oil, 2 tablespoons butter, and zest and juice of ½ lemon gently. Add the pasta, reserved water, and toss. Sprinkle with ¼ teaspoon thyme leaves.

ANCHOVIES

Fry 1 diced garlic clove in 3 tablespoons extra-virgin olive oil until fragrant. Add 4 chopped anchovies and stir for 2 minutes. Add the pasta, reserved water, and toss. Season and sprinkle with chopped parsley.

DITALINI WITH BORLOTTI BEANS

SERVES : 2
PREP : 10 MINS
COOK : 15 MINS

INGREDIENTS

2 tablespoons extra-virgin olive oil, plus extra for drizzling

1 garlic clove, lightly crushed

1 ounce (30g) pancetta, diced

10½ ounces (300g) soffritto (page 10)

1 tablespoon strained pureed tomatoes (passata)

1 (15-ounce / 425g) can borlotti beans, washed

6¾ ounces (190g) dried ditalini

salt and pepper

1 tablespoon chopped herbs, for serving

Pasta e fagioli, the Italian beans and pasta, is a typical dish from the "cucina povera," a cuisine always focused on well-balanced, filling dishes made with simple pantry ingredients. This is a typical peasant recipe because beans are more plentiful and cheaper than meat, though still packed with protein.

1. Heat the oil in a large saucepan, add the garlic, pancetta, and soffritto, and brown for a few minutes. Add the strained pureed tomatoes, stir for a few seconds, then add the beans. Stir for 2 minutes before adding 2 cups (500ml) boiling water. Season and bring to a boil.

2. Add the pasta to the pan and cook, stirring frequently, for 1 minute less than the package directions, adding little more boiling water, if necessary. Remove the garlic from the pan and discard. Let the pasta rest for 5 minutes before serving with a drizzle of oil, some black pepper, and chopped herbs.

PASTA AND PEAS

SERVES: 2
PREP: 5 MINS
COOK: 20 MINS

INGREDIENTS

2 tablespoons extra-virgin
olive oil

½ onion, finely diced

1¾ ounces (50g)
pancetta, diced

5 cherry tomatoes, halved

1¼ cups (150g)
fresh or frozen peas

⅓ pound (150g)
dried conchiglie

salt

grated Parmesan cheese,
for sprinkling

This Neapolitan-style recipe is a cross
between a soup and a pasta dish. Fresh
or frozen peas cook quickly, making this
an easy dinner when you are short on time.

1. Heat the oil in a large saucepan, add the onion and
pancetta, and cook for 3 minutes. Add the tomatoes,
stir for 1 minute, then add the peas together with 2 cups
(500ml) boiling water. Bring to a gentle boil, then simmer
for about 5 minutes. Season with salt.

2. Add the pasta to the pan and cook gently, stirring
frequently, for 1 minute less than the package directions,
adding little more boiling water, if necessary. Serve with
grated Parmesan.

MUSHROOM AND POTATO PASTA SOUP

SERVES: 2
PREP: 25 MINS
COOK: 30 MINS

INGREDIENTS

1 cup (20g) dried
porcini mushrooms

2 tablespoons extra-virgin
olive oil

10½ ounces (300g)
soffritto (page 10)

7 ounces (200g) mixed
mushrooms, cleaned
and diced

3½ ounces (100g)
potatoes, diced

1 bouquet garni of thyme
and parsley

⅓ pound (150g)
dried spaghetti, broken

salt

Mushroom and potato pasta soup is a healthy
vegetarian comfort food. The addition of
dried porcini mushrooms gives this comforting
dish a real umami flavor boost.

1. Soak the porcini in a small bowl of hot water
for 15 minutes. Drain the porcini, chop them finely,
and set aside their liquid.

2. Heat the oil in a large saucepan over medium to
high heat, add the soffritto, and sauté for a few minutes.
Add the mushrooms, chopped porcini, and potatoes and
fry for 2 minutes, stirring occasionally. Add the bouquet
garni, the porcini liquid, and 2 cups (500ml) boiling
water. Season with salt and cook for 20 minutes.

3. Add the pasta to the pan and cook for 1 minute less
than the package directions. Serve hot.

ONE-POT LASAGNA

SERVES: 2
PREP: 5 MINS
COOK: 30 MINS

INGREDIENTS

2 tablespoons extra-virgin olive oil

10½ ounces (300g) soffritto (page 10)

½ cup (100g) ground beef

½ cup (100g) ground pork

1 cup (200g) strained pureed tomatoes (passata)

4 fresh lasagna sheets, halved

4½ ounces (125g) mozzarella, sliced

grated Parmesan cheese, for sprinkling

salt

basil leaves, for garnishing

As the title suggests, this is the easiest lasagna you will ever make. If you are vegetarian then use your favorite mushrooms instead of the ground meat.

1. Heat the oil in a large ovenproof saucepan over medium heat, add the soffritto, and sauté for 3 minutes. Add the ground meat and cook, breaking up the meat with a wooden spoon, until browned. Pour in the strained pureed tomatoes, then season with salt and cook for 15 minutes.

2. Preheat the broiler.

3. Add 1 cup (200ml) boiling water, then add the lasagna sheets and simmer, stirring occasionally, until the pasta is soft and cooked halfway through. Fold the lasagna sheets in on themselves in the pan, then place the mozzarella slices between them and on top. Sprinkle the Parmesan over the top and broil for 5 minutes, or until the edges are crispy. Let stand for 2 minutes before serving, garnished with basil.

CREAMY PUMPKIN PASTA

SERVES: 2
PREP: 5 MINS
COOK: 25 MINS

INGREDIENTS

2 tablespoons extra-virgin olive oil

½ onion, finely chopped

1 ounce (30g) pancetta, diced

1 medium pumpkin or squash, peeled, seeded, and cut into 1¼-inch (3cm) cubes

1 rosemary sprig

¼ cup (50g) mascarpone cheese

5 ounces (140g) dried rigatoni

grated Parmesan cheese, for sprinkling

salt and pepper

The pumpkin is the protagonist of this delicious dish with an irresistible creamy and rich flavor. Combined with mascarpone, it turns into a silky pasta sauce.

1. Heat the oil in a large saucepan over low to medium heat, add the onion, and sauté for 3 minutes. Add the pancetta and fry until crispy, then remove from the pan and set aside.

2. Add the pumpkin and rosemary to the pan together with 1 cup (200ml) boiling water. Season with salt and pepper and cook for 10 minutes.

3. Remove the rosemary sprig and discard, then transfer half of the pumpkin to a mixer and blitz until it is creamy. Add the mascarpone cheese, mix well, adding a splash of water if necessary, and set aside.

4. Add the pasta to the pan with the remaining pumpkin. Pour in enough boiling water to cover the pasta and cook for 1 minute less than the package directions. When cooked, add the pumpkin and mascarpone mixture to the pan. Toss and mix until everything is combined. Season to taste. Sprinkle with Parmesan and serve with the crispy pancetta on top.

GREENS AND SEAFOOD MINESTRA

SERVES: 2
PREP: 35 MINS
COOK: 30 MINS

This mixed greens and seafood minestra is a soup of true elegance. Incredibly vibrant, it is full of flavor and looks as good as it tastes.

INGREDIENTS

10½ ounces (300g) mussels

2 tablespoons extra-virgin olive oil, plus extra for drizzling

1 garlic clove, crushed

10½ ounces (300g) mixed greens (escarole, chard), coarsely chopped

2 ounces (60g) dried cavatappi

1¾ ounces (50g) mixed ripe tomatoes, halved

salt and pepper

finely chopped parsley, for garnishing

1. Wash the mussels, then soak them in a large bowl of salted water for 30 minutes. Wash them again, then let drain. Discard any mussels that are open.

2. Heat the oil in a large saucepan with a lid, add the garlic, and fry for 1 minute. Add the mussels, cover tightly, and shake the pan until the mussels are open. Discard any mussels that have not opened. Remove them from the pan and strain the cooking liquid through a fine-mesh strainer into a bowl. Remove all the mussels from their shells and set aside.

3. In the same saucepan, heat the seafood liquid with 1¾ cups (400ml) boiling water. Bring to a boil, then add the greens and cook for 10 minutes. Add the pasta and after 8 minutes, add the mussels and tomatoes, and cook for 2 minutes. Season with salt and pepper, drizzle with oil, and garnish with parsley before serving.

LINGUINE WITH CHERRY TOMATOES

SERVES: 2
PREP: 5 MINS
COOK: 15 MINS

INGREDIENTS

6 ounces (180g) dried linguine

1 cup (180g) cherry tomatoes, halved

2 tablespoons extra-virgin olive oil

1 garlic clove, diced

1 handful of basil

grated Parmesan cheese, for sprinkling

salt

This recipe uses an innovative technique as all the ingredients are cooked together in the same pan with cold water. As the pasta cooks, it releases starch, which helps to make the sauce creamier. The addition of the cheese and basil gives this dish a wonderful flavor. Don't add too much water as you don't want to overcook the pasta.

1. Combine all the ingredients, except the Parmesan, in a large saucepan and add 2 cups (480ml) water. Bring to a boil over high heat and cook, stirring and turning the pasta until it is al dente and the water has completely evaporated. Season with salt, sprinkle with Parmesan, and mix to combine before serving.

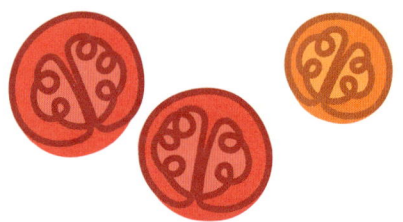

FREGULA WITH CLAMS

SERVES: 2
PREP: 35 MINS
COOK: 25 MINS

INGREDIENTS

1 pound (500g) clams

¼ cup (60ml) extra-virgin olive oil

1 garlic clove, lightly crushed

½ red chile, chopped

a splash of white wine

4½ ounces (125g) dried fregula

salt and pepper

chopped parsley, for garnishing

A traditional dish from the island of Sardinia, this combines a small, round, toasted pasta similar to couscous, with clams all cooked in a flavorful broth. Ideal for fish dishes or light soups, fregula has a unique flavor due to its drying and toasting process.

1. Wash the clams, then soak them in a large bowl of salted water for 30 minutes. Wash them again, then let drain.

2. Heat 2 tablespoons of the oil in a large, deep skillet with a lid, add the garlic, and fry for 1 minute. Add the clams, cover tightly, and shake the pan until all the clams are open. Remove the clams from the pan and strain the cooking liquid through a fine-mesh strainer into a bowl. Remove half of the clams from the shell and set aside.

3. In the same pan, heat the remaining oil over medium heat, add the chile, and fry gently for 1 minute. Add the wine and simmer for 2 minutes.

4. Add the reserved cooking liquid to the pan and bring to a boil. Add the fregula and cook, stirring occasionally, for 12 minutes. If the mixture becomes too thick add a little boiling water.

5. After 12 minutes, add the clams, with and without the shells, and cook for 2 minutes. Season to taste and garnish with parsley before serving.

BAKE IN
THE OVEN

VEGETABLE PASTA GRATIN

SERVES : 2
PREP : 10 MINS
COOK : 35 MINS

INGREDIENTS

½ head of broccoli, chopped

2 medium carrots, diced

1 small zucchini, sliced

6 ounces (180g) dried fusilli

½ cup (125g) ricotta cheese

4 tablespoons grated Parmesan cheese

scant 1 cup (200ml) half and half (single cream)

1 teaspoon thyme leaves, plus thyme sprigs for garnishing

1¾ ounces (50g) spinach

½ small mozzarella, torn

2 tablespoons extra-virgin olive oil

salt and pepper

This recipe is packed with fresh vegetables, including spinach, broccoli, carrots, and zucchini. It is a perfect filling comfort food for vegetarians and meat-eaters alike.

1. Preheat the oven to 350°F (180°C).

2. Bring a large saucepan of lightly salted water to a boil, add the broccoli and carrots, and cook for 2 minutes. Add the zucchini and pasta and cook for 3 minutes less than the package directions.

3. Meanwhile, place the ricotta in a large bowl, add 2 tablespoons of the Parmesan, the cream and thyme, and mix to combine. Season with salt and pepper.

4. One minute before the pasta is ready, add the spinach to the pan, then drain and mix together with the ricotta sauce and mozzarella.

5. Transfer the pasta to an ovenproof dish, sprinkle the remaining Parmesan over the top, then drizzle with the oil. Bake for 25 minutes. Rest for 2 minutes before serving, garnished with thyme sprigs.

SORRENTO-STYLE CANNELLONI

SERVES : 2 + LEFTOVERS
PREP : 10 MINS
COOK : 20 MINS

INGREDIENTS

2 ¼ cups (500g)
good-quality ricotta
cheese, drained

9 ounces (250g)
mozzarella, diced

2 ¼ cups (150g)
grated Parmesan cheese

few basil leaves

1 quantity of Fresh Tomato
Sauce (page 43)

20 dried cannelloni tubes

salt and pepper

This version of the classic cannelloni is typical of the city of Sorrento. It is easy to make and you can keep a few portions in the freezer. If you can't find ready-made cannelloni you can use sheets of fresh lasagna (cut into 4 by 8 inch / 10 by 20cm pieces) and roll them into tubes to enclose the filling.

1. Preheat the oven to 400°F (200°C).

2. Mash the ricotta in a large bowl with a fork. Add ⅓ pound (150g) of the mozzarella, 1 ½ cups (100g) of the Parmesan cheese, a few basil leaves, and season with salt and pepper.

3. Spread 2 tablespoons of the tomato sauce in the bottom of a large ovenproof dish.

4. Fill a pastry bag with the ricotta mixture and use to fill each of the cannelloni tubes right to the top. Place the cannelloni tubes into the prepared dish, cover with the rest of the tomato sauce, and top with the remaining mozzarella, Parmesan, and basil.

5. Bake for 20 minutes, or until golden brown and bubbling. Serve hot.

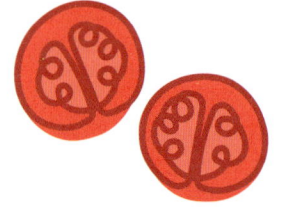

STUFFED CONCHIGLIONI

SERVES: 2

PREP: 5 MINS

COOK: 30 MINS

INGREDIENTS

2 tablespoons extra-virgin
olive oil

1 garlic clove,
lightly crushed

1 (15-ounce / 425g)
can chopped tomatoes

6 ounces (180g)
dried conchiglioni

5 cups (250g) spinach

½ cup (125g)
ricotta cheese

1 egg

generous pinch of
grated nutmeg

grated Parmesan cheese,
for sprinkling

salt and pepper

Conchiglioni are the biggest of the shell
family. Beautiful and easy to prepare, the
shape of the pasta holds the creamy ricotta
and spinach filling perfectly.

1. Preheat the oven to 350°F (180°C).

2. Heat the oil in a saucepan over medium heat, add the
garlic, and cook until fragrant. Add the tomatoes, season
to taste with salt and pepper, and cook for 5 minutes.
Remove and discard the garlic.

3. At the same time, bring a large saucepan of water to
a boil, add salt, then the pasta, and cook the pasta for
4 minutes less than the package directions. Drain and
set aside.

4. Meanwhile, blanch the spinach in boiling water for
2 minutes, drain, chop coarsely, and place in a large
bowl. Add the ricotta, egg, nutmeg, and 1 tablespoon
of the Parmesan, and mix to combine.

5. Spread a layer of the tomato sauce in the bottom
of a 9½-inch (24cm) ovenproof dish. Fill the conchiglioni
with the spinach and ricotta mixture and arrange the
stuffed pasta in the dish, open-side up. Spoon over the
rest of the tomato sauce and sprinkle with the remaining
Parmesan. Bake for 20 minutes. Serve at once.

RIGATONI CAKE

SERVES : 2 + LEFTOVERS
PREP : 5 MINS
COOK : 60 MINS

Oven-baked pasta is the ultimate comfort food, so impress and satisfy your family with this stunning showstopper for your table.

INGREDIENTS

2 tablespoons olive oil

10½ ounces (300g) soffritto (page 10)

½ cup (120g) ground beef

½ cup (120g) ground pork

1⅔ cups (360g) strained pureed tomatoes (passata)

14 ounces (400g) dried rigatoni

1 quantity of Béchamel Sauce (page 157)

grated Parmesan cheese, for sprinkling

salt

1. Heat the oil in a saucepan over medium heat, add the soffritto, and sauté for about 3 minutes. Add the ground meat and cook until browned, breaking up the meat with a wooden spoon as you stir. Add the strained pureed tomatoes, season with salt, and cook for 30 minutes.

2. Meanwhile, bring a large saucepan of water to a boil, add salt, then add the pasta and cook for 4 minutes less than the package directions. Drain the pasta, being careful not to break them, and set aside.

3. Preheat the oven to 375°F (190°C).

4. Use half of the meat sauce to coat the rigatoni.

5. Line the bottom and sides of a 7-inch (18cm) springform cake pan with baking parchment. Arrange the pasta vertically in the prepared pan and spread the remaining meat sauce over the top. Spread the béchamel sauce over and sprinkle with the Parmesan. Bake for 20 minutes, or until the top is golden. Let cool for a few minutes before serving.

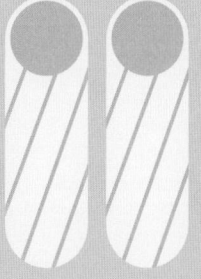

LASAGNA ROLLS

SERVES: 2 + LEFTOVERS
PREP: 10 MINS
COOK: 20 MINS

INGREDIENTS

2 tablespoons extra-virgin olive oil

1 garlic clove, lightly crushed

5 cups (250g) spinach

1 cup (250g) ricotta cheese

1 generous pinch of grated nutmeg

1 quantity of Fresh Tomato Sauce (page 43)

4 fresh lasagna sheets, each sheet 6¼ by 8½ inches (16 by 22cm)

7 ounces (200g) prosciutto

grated Parmesan cheese, for sprinkling

salt and pepper

These lasagna rolls with ricotta and spinach are one of the many ways of reinventing lasagna noodles. Simply add the filling to the lasagna sheets and roll up.

1. Preheat the oven to 350°F (180°C).

2. Heat the oil in a large skillet with a lid, add the garlic, and fry until fragrant. Add the spinach, cover, and cook for 4 minutes. Remove the garlic, drain the spinach juice from the pan, and chop the spinach coarsely.

3. Mix the spinach and ricotta together in a large bowl. Season with salt, pepper, and nutmeg.

4. Spread half of the tomato sauce over the bottom of a 9 by 13-inch (23 by 33cm) ovenproof dish.

5. Take a lasagna sheet, spread with a spoonful of the ricotta and spinach mixture, add a slice of prosciutto, and roll up from the short side. Cut into four with a serrated knife and repeat the process with the remaining lasagna sheets and filling until they are all used up. Arrange the rolls in the dish, cover with the remaining tomato sauce, and sprinkle the Parmesan over the top. Bake for 15 minutes. Serve hot.

TASTY MAC AND CHEESE

SERVES: 2 + LEFTOVERS
PREP: 5 MINS
COOK: 45 MINS

INGREDIENTS

3 tablespoons butter, plus extra for greasing

4 tablespoons fresh breadcrumbs

3½ tablespoons all-purpose flour

2 cups (500ml) milk

1 generous pinch of grated nutmeg

3½ cups (400g) grated mixed cheese, such as Fontina and Emmental

14 ounces (400g) dried small cavatappi

grated Parmesan cheese, for sprinkling

salt and pepper

In Italy, this dish is called pasta gratin with more elaborate versions adding vegetables, ham, or sausage. The pasta is mixed in a cheese sauce, then Parmesan is sprinkled on top to create a crunchy crust in the oven. This dish freezes well so double up the ingredients and make one for another time.

1. Preheat the oven to 400°F (200°C). Lightly grease a shallow ovenproof dish with butter and cover the bottom and sides with 2 tablespoons of the breadcrumbs.

2. Melt the butter in a small saucepan over low heat. Sprinkle in the flour and mix to create a light-colored thick paste (roux). Cook for 1 minute, then slowly add the milk in batches and whisk thoroughly to break up the lumps. Add the nutmeg, salt, pepper, and grated cheeses and cook gently for 10 minutes, or until it begins to thicken and become glossy.

3. Meanwhile, bring a large saucepan of water to a boil, add salt, then the pasta, and cook for 4 minutes less than the package directions. Drain the pasta and put into a heatproof bowl. Add the sauce and mix to combine.

4. Pour the mixture into the prepared dish, sprinkle with the grated Parmesan and the remaining breadcrumbs, and bake for 30 minutes, or until crisp and golden brown. Let cool for a few minutes before serving.

EGGPLANT PASTA BAKE

SERVES: 2 + LEFTOVERS
PREP: 5 MINS
COOK: 30 MINS

INGREDIENTS

¾ cup (180ml)
sunflower oil

1 garlic clove,
lightly crushed

2 eggplants, diced into
½-inch (1cm) cubes

¾ pound (350g)
dried penne

1 quantity of Fresh Tomato
Sauce (page 43)

9 ounces (250g)
mozzarella, diced

grated Parmesan cheese,
for sprinkling

salt

basil leaves, for garnishing

Baked pasta is one of the most popular dishes in Italy and this version is simple. You can replace the Parmesan with a vegetarian Italian hard cheese, if desired.

1. Preheat the oven to 350°F (180°C).

2. Heat the oil in a large pan over medium heat, add the garlic, and cook until fragrant. Add the eggplant and cook until soft and golden brown. Remove and discard the garlic.

3. Meanwhile, bring a large saucepan of water to a boil, add salt, then the pasta, and cook the pasta for 4 minutes less than the package directions.

4. When the pasta is cooked, drain and add it back to the pan. Add the tomato sauce, two-thirds of the eggplant, and two-thirds of the mozzarella, and mix well to combine.

5. Pour the mixture into a large ovenproof dish and top with the remaining mozzarella and eggplants. Sprinkle with the Parmesan and bake for 20 minutes, or until golden brown. Serve hot, garnished with basil.

BÉCHAMEL SAUCE

CHEESY BÉCHAMEL SAUCE

HERB BÉCHAMEL SAUCE

BÉCHAMEL SAUCE WITH TRUFFLE

BÉCHAMEL SAUCE FOUR WAYS

BÉCHAMEL SAUCE

MAKES : 10½ OUNCES (300G)

PREP : 5 MINS

COOK : 12 MINS

Béchamel, known as *besciamella* in Italian, is a classic sauce that can elevate a dish. Store it in the refrigerator for up to three days.

INGREDIENTS

2 tablespoons butter

2 tablespoons all-purpose flour

1 cup (250ml) milk, warm

generous pinch of grated nutmeg

salt and pepper

1. Melt the butter in a saucepan over low heat. Sprinkle in the flour and mix to create a light-colored thick paste (roux). Cook for 1 minute.

2. Slowly add the milk in batches and whisk thoroughly to break up the lumps. Add the nutmeg, salt, and pepper and cook gently for 10 minutes, or until it begins to thicken and become glossy.

CHEESY BÉCHAMEL SAUCE

Make the sauce above, then add ½ cup (50g) grated Gruyère and 2 tablespoons grated Parmesan. Stir until melted, adding a splash of milk if too thick.

HERB BÉCHAMEL SAUCE

Start making the sauce above. After stirring in the milk, add a bay leaf, 1 tablespoon chopped mixed herbs, and salt and pepper. Cook for 10 minutes. Discard the bay.

BÉCHAMEL SAUCE WITH TRUFFLE

Make the sauce above using 2 tablespoons truffle butter. Insert a clove into ¼ onion and add to the sauce. Season. Cook for 10 minutes. Discard the onion before serving.

THE MIGHTY LASAGNA BOLOGNESE

SERVES: 2 + LEFTOVERS
PREP: 10 MINS
COOK: 25 MINS

This rich and tasty recipe from the Emilia Romagna region of Italy is one of the most iconic dishes in Italian cuisine, and it is appreciated and made all around the world.

INGREDIENTS

1 quantity of Béchamel Sauce (page 157)

2 (1-pound / 500g) packages dried lasagna sheets

1 quantity of Bolognese Sauce (page 25)

grated Parmesan cheese, for sprinkling

1. Preheat the oven to 350°F (180°C).

2. Spread a thin layer of béchamel sauce on the bottom of a 9 by 13-inch (23 by 33cm) ovenproof dish.

3. Arrange a layer of lasagna sheets on top of the béchamel sauce, don't worry if they overlap, then top with a layer of Bolognese sauce followed by more béchamel sauce, combining both with the back of a spoon. Sprinkle with some of the Parmesan and repeat the layers until all the ingredients have been used up and finishing with the cheese.

4. Bake for 25 minutes or until golden brown. Let stand for 5 minutes before serving.

PUMPKIN LASAGNA

SERVES: 2 + LEFTOVERS
PREP: 10 MINS
COOK: 65 MINS

The sweet and earthy flavor of pumpkin is the winning ingredient in this fall-inspired comfort food.

INGREDIENTS

4 tablespoons butter

4 sage leaves

¼ onion, thinly sliced

1 small pumpkin, about 1 pound (500g), peeled, seeded, and cut into 1¼-inch (3cm) cubes

1 quantity of Béchamel Sauce (page 157)

2 (1-pound / 500g) dried packages lasagna sheets

14 ounces (400g) mozzarella, diced

grated Parmesan cheese, for sprinkling

salt and pepper

1. Preheat the oven to 350°F (180°C).

2. Melt the butter in a large saucepan and gently fry the sage leaves for about 2 minutes. Add the onion and sauté for 5 minutes.

3. Add the pumpkin, cook for 1 minute, then add ¼ cup (60ml) boiling water and simmer for 30 minutes, stirring occasionally, or until you can mash the pumpkin with a fork. Season with salt and pepper.

4. Spread a thin layer of béchamel sauce over the bottom of a 9 by 13-inch (23 by 33cm) ovenproof dish.

5. Arrange a layer of lasagna sheets over the top of the béchamel sauce, don't worry if they overlap. Spread another layer of béchamel sauce, followed by some of the pumpkin and mozzarella. Sprinkle with some Parmesan and repeat the process until all the ingredients are used up, and finishing with a sprinkling of Parmesan.

6. Bake for 25 minutes, or until golden brown. Let stand for 5 minutes before serving.

VEGETABLE LASAGNA

SERVES: 2 + LEFTOVERS
PREP: 10 MINS
COOK: 35 MINS

INGREDIENTS

¼ cup (60ml) olive oil

1 onion, thinly sliced

2 carrots, julienned

1 small broccoli head, cut into florets, and stalk peeled and julienned

2 zucchini, julienned

7 ounces (200g) mushrooms, sliced

2 quantities of Béchamel Sauce (page 157)

1 (1 pound / 500g) package dried lasagna sheets

grated Parmesan cheese, for sprinkling (optional)

salt and pepper

This dish is a lighter and more colorful version of the classic lasagna, but is still delicious, comforting, and filling. You can use any vegetables you have, so it's a sort of refrigerator-cleanout recipe too.

1. Preheat the oven to 350°F (180°C).

2. Heat the oil in a large skillet, add the onion, and gently sauté for 3 minutes. Add the carrots and broccoli and cook for a few minutes with a splash of water, then add the zucchini and mushrooms. Season with salt and pepper and cook until all the vegetables are tender.

3. Spread a thin layer of the béchamel sauce on the bottom of a 9 by 13-inch (23 by 33cm) ovenproof dish.

4. Arrange a layer of lasagna sheets on top of the béchamel sauce, don't worry if they overlap. Top with another layer of béchamel sauce, followed by spoonfuls of the vegetables. Repeat the process until all the ingredients have been used up.

5. Bake for 25 minutes, or until golden brown. Let stand for 5 minutes before serving, then sprinkle with the grated Parmesan, if desired.

BAKED ZITI

SERVES: 2 + LEFTOVERS
PREP: 5 MINS
COOK: 40 MINS

This recipe, mostly made from pantry ingredients, is perfect for when you don't have much time available but also don't want to give up on flavor.

INGREDIENTS

6 tablespoons extra-virgin olive oil

1 garlic clove

3 Italian sausages, skins removed

2 cups (500ml) strained pureed tomatoes (passata)

¾ pound (350g) dried ziti

9 ounces (250g) scamorza cheese, diced

grated Parmesan cheese, for sprinkling

salt and pepper

1. Preheat the oven to 350°F (180°C).

2. Heat the oil in a large saucepan over medium heat, add the garlic, and cook until fragrant. Add the sausage and cook for 8 minutes, breaking up with the back of a spoon, until browned. Add the strained pureed tomatoes and cook for another 10 minutes. Remove and discard the garlic and season with salt and pepper.

3. Meanwhile, bring a large pan of water to a boil, add salt, then the pasta, and cook for 4 minutes less than the package directions. When cooked, drain and add back to the saucepan. Add the tomato and sausage mixture and two-thirds of the scamorza and mix well to combine.

4. Pour the mixture into a 9½-inch (24cm) ovenproof dish, top with the remaining scamorza, sprinkle the Parmesan over the top, and bake for 20 minutes, or until golden brown. Serve hot, sprinkled with extra grated Parmesan.

CREAMY TOMATO AND BURRATA BAKE

SERVES: 2 + LEFTOVERS
PREP: 5 MINS
COOK: 45 MINS

INGREDIENTS

2 tablespoons extra-virgin olive oil

1 garlic clove, lightly crushed

2 (15-ounce / 425g) cans plum tomatoes, coarsely chopped

2 basil sprigs, leaves picked and chopped

11 ½ ounces (320g) dried rigatoni

7 ounces (200g) burrata

grated Pecorino Romano cheese, for sprinkling

salt and pepper

This baked pasta, with its delicious crust and soft cheese, is quick and easy. It can be prepared in advance and cooked an hour before serving.

1. Heat the oil in a large saucepan, add the garlic, and fry until fragrant. Add the tomatoes, half of the basil, and season with salt and pepper. Cook for about 20 minutes. Remove and discard the garlic.

2. Preheat the oven to 350°F (180°C).

3. Meanwhile, bring a large saucepan of water to a boil, add salt, then the pasta, and cook for 4 minutes less than the package directions. When cooked, drain and add the pasta back to the saucepan. Add two-thirds of the tomato sauce and mix well to combine.

4. Pour the mixture into a large ovenproof dish, spoon over the remaining sauce, then add the burrata in pieces and sprinkle the pecorino and remaining chopped basil over the top. Bake for 25 minutes, or until golden brown. Let stand for 5 minutes before serving.

SICILIAN TIMBALLO

SERVES: 2 + LEFTOVERS
PREP: 30 MINS
COOK: 65 MINS

One of the quintessential dishes from Sicily, this rich and substantial recipe uses a specific pasta shape called anelletti, which is perfect for baking as it copes well with cooking for a long time.

INGREDIENTS

2 tablespoons extra-virgin olive oil, plus extra for greasing

10½ ounces (300g) soffritto (page 10)

1 cup (250g) ground pork

2½ cups (600ml) strained pureed tomatoes (passata)

¾ cup (100g) peas

1¾ cups (400ml) sunflower oil

2 eggplants, sliced

2 tablespoons fresh breadcrumbs

7 ounces (200g) dried anelletti

7 ounces (200g) provolone or semihard cow's milk cheese, diced

2 hard-boiled eggs, quartered

grated Parmesan cheese, for sprinkling

salt and pepper

1. Heat the olive oil in a large pan, add the soffritto, and sauté for 3 minutes. Add the pork and brown evenly for 5 minutes. Add the strained pureed tomatoes and season. Cook for 30 minutes. After 25 minutes, add the peas.

2. Sprinkle the eggplants with salt, place them in a colander, and let stand for 15 minutes. Rinse the eggplants and pat dry with paper towels. Heat the sunflower oil in a large, deep skillet. Add the eggplants and fry until golden brown. Drain on paper towels.

3. Preheat the oven to 350°F (180°C). Grease an 8½-inch (22cm) springform pan with oil, then sprinkle it with breadcrumbs. Starting from the edge, line the eggplant slices vertically round the sides, then lay the slices over the bottom of the pan to cover.

4. Bring a large pan of water to a boil, add salt, then the pasta, and cook for 2 minutes less than the package directions. Drain and add back to the pan. Mix in most of the sauce, setting aside ¼ cup (60ml) and two-thirds of the diced cheese. Pour half of the mixture into the pan, top with the eggs, remaining diced cheese, and sprinkle with Parmesan. Cover with the remaining pasta mixture, then spoon over the rest of the sauce. Bake for 25 minutes. Leave for 5 minutes before serving.

USING UP
LEFTOVERS

FRITTATA

SERVES: 2 + LEFTOVERS
PREP: 5 MINS
COOK: 10 MINS

INGREDIENTS

6 eggs, beaten

½ cup (40g) Pecorino Romano cheese, grated

1 tablespoon chopped parsley

14 ounces (400g) cooked spaghetti

¼ cup (60ml) olive oil

salt and pepper

Pasta frittata is one of the greatest ways of using up any leftover pasta shapes you may have in the pantry and any produce left in the refrigerator; just think of pasta and eggs as the base of multiple creations.

1. Mix the eggs, cheese, parsley, and salt and pepper to taste together in a large bowl. Add the spaghetti and stir to combine.

2. Heat the oil in a nonstick pan with a lid, add the egg mixture, distribute it evenly over the bottom, cover with the lid, and cook gently for 5 minutes.

3. Shake the pan to release the frittata from the bottom, then place a plate the same size as the pan on top and carefully turn the pan upside down. Return the frittata to the pan and cook for another 5 minutes. Turn the frittata one more time and finish cooking for another 5 minutes. Eat straight away or cold.

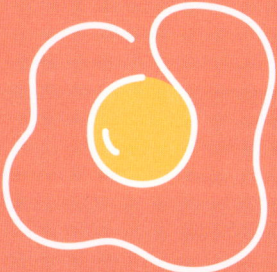

CREAMY POTATO AND CHEESE PASTA

SERVES: 2

PREP: 5 MINS

COOK: 30 MINS

INGREDIENTS

2 tablespoons extra-virgin olive oil

10½ ounces (300g) soffritto (page 10)

2 ounces (60g) pancetta, diced

1 tablespoon strained pureed tomatoes (passata)

¾ pound (350g) potatoes, peeled and diced

5 ounces (140g) dried pasta mista

2¾ ounces (80g) smoked provola cheese, diced

salt and pepper

The richest version of this dish is the Neapolitan, where smoked provola cheese is added to create the ultimate comfort food. In Naples, it is associated with "pasta mista," a charming collection of different pasta shapes left over from the manufacturing process. If you can't find pasta mista then use a variety of leftover pasta you have in the pantry.

1. Heat the oil in a large saucepan, add the soffritto, pancetta, and strained pureed tomatoes, and fry for a few minutes. Add the diced potatoes, stir, and cook for a minute before adding 2 cups (500ml) hot water. Season with salt.

2. Cook gently for 15 to 20 minutes until the potatoes are soft. Add a glass of hot water, then add the pasta, bring back to a boil, and cook the pasta until it is al dente, adding more water if needed.

3. Remove the pan from the heat, add the provola, season to taste, and let rest for a few minutes before serving. The result should be creamy.

PIZZA PASTA

SERVES: 2
PREP: 5 MINS
COOK: 10 MINS

It's very quick and easy to prepare this "pizza" as you are using up either leftover plain pasta or sauced pasta, or even both.

INGREDIENTS

10½ ounces (300g) cooked spaghetti or linguine

2 tablespoons extra-virgin olive oil, plus extra for drizzling

1 quantity of Marinara Sauce (page 43)

1 small mozzarella, sliced

1 basil sprig, leaves picked

salt and pepper

1. Add the pasta, 2 tablespoons of the oil, and half of the marinara sauce to a large bowl and season to taste.

2. Preheat the oven to 400°F (200°C). Line a large sheet pan with baking parchment.

3. Drizzle some oil on the prepared sheet pan and pour the mixture into the pan, leveling and shaping it into a circle. Spread over the remaining sauce, then top with the mozzarella and basil. Bake for 10 minutes, or until the mozzarella is melted. Serve hot.

USING UP LEFTOVERS

EGGPLANT ROLLS

SERVES: 2
PREP: 25 MINS
COOK: 15 MINS

INGREDIENTS

2 medium eggplants, cut into ¼-inch (5mm) thick slices

1¼ cups (300ml) sunflower oil

20 cherry tomatoes, quartered

1 basil sprig, leaves picked and torn

2 tablespoons grated Parmesan cheese

4½ ounces (130g) cooked linguine or spaghetti

2 tablespoons extra-virgin olive oil

salt

These eggplant rolls are a reinterpretation of the Sicilian "pasta alla Norma," with the eggplants that wrap the pasta transforming into delicious yet simple-to-prepare rolls. Use either leftover cooked spaghetti or linguine in this recipe.

1. Sprinkle the sliced eggplants with salt, place them in a colander, and let stand for 15 minutes to remove their bitterness. Rinse the eggplants under cold running water, then pat dry with paper towels.

2. Heat the sunflower oil in a nonstick skillet. Add the eggplants and cook them for a few minutes on each side. Lay them out on a sheet of baking parchment.

3. Preheat the oven to 350°F (180°C).

4. Mix two-thirds of the tomatoes, the basil, 1 tablespoon of the Parmesan, and the pasta together in a medium bowl. Drizzle with 1 tablespoon of the olive oil and toss to combine. Season to taste. Put a forkful of the spaghetti mixture over each eggplant slice and roll up.

5. Arrange the rolls, with the sealed-side facing downwards, in a 9 by 13-inch (23 by 33cm) ovenproof dish. Drizzle with the remaining oil, then sprinkle with the remaining Parmesan, and add the rest of the tomatoes over the top. Bake for 10 minutes, or until golden brown. Serve hot.

FRITTERS

SERVES : 2
PREP : 15 MINS
COOK : 5 MINS

INGREDIENTS

6 ounces (180g) cooked long pasta

scant ½ cup (100ml) olive oil

1 tablespoon dried breadcrumbs

1 tablespoon mixed dried herbs

½ cup (120ml) sunflower oil

salt and pepper

These fritters are perfect for using up leftover spaghetti or other long pasta as finger food with cured meats.

1. Line a large baking sheet with baking parchment. Mix the pasta, olive oil, breadcrumbs, herbs, and salt and pepper to taste together in a large bowl.

2. Twist about 1 ounce (30g) spaghetti like a nest with a fork, arrange on the prepared baking sheet, and let rest in the refrigerator for 10 minutes.

3. Heat the sunflower oil in a large skillet and fry each nest for 2 minutes, or until crisp and golden on one side. Turn over and cook the other side for another 2 minutes. Serve hot.

CROQUETTES

SERVES: 2

PREP: 70 MINS

COOK: 10 MINS

INGREDIENTS

6 ounces (180g) cooked pasta, coarsely chopped

1 egg, lightly beaten

2 tablespoons grated Parmesan cheese

2 tablespoons fresh breadcrumbs

1¾ ounces (50g) scamorza cheese, cubed

scant ½ cup (100ml) sunflower oil

salt and pepper

The perfect bite to have with an aperitif. Enjoy the croquettes as they are or pair them with your favorite dip. I love to eat them with olive pâté and sundried tomato pesto.

1. Mix the pasta, egg, Parmesan, and 1 tablespoon breadcrumbs together in a medium bowl. Season to taste. Line a large baking sheet with baking parchment. Take a spoonful of the mixture and place it on the prepared sheet. Continue until all the mixture is used up. Let chill in the refrigerator for at least 1 hour.

2. Using your hands, shape the mixture into croquettes and insert a few cubes of cheese into the middle of each one.

3. Heat the oil in a large saucepan. When hot, dip each croquette into the remaining breadcrumbs and carefully add to the hot oil. Fry for 3 to 4 minutes until golden and crisp, then remove, drain on paper towels, and serve.

PASTA SALAD

SERVES : 2

PREP : 70 MINS

COOK : 10 MINS

INGREDIENTS

²⁄₃ cup (150ml)
extra-virgin olive oil,
plus extra for drizzling

1 garlic clove, slightly
crushed

1 eggplant, diced

1 yellow bell pepper,
diced

1 zucchini, diced

10 mixed tomatoes,
quartered

1 basil sprig, leaves
picked

¹⁄₃ pound (150g) cooked
penne

salt and pepper

Salad is one of the easiest ways of reusing leftovers. In this recipe, I've used leftover cooked penne and summer vegetables that needed eating, but you can change the vegetables according to the season.

1. Heat the oil in a nonstick pan, add the garlic, and fry for 2 minutes. Add the eggplant and cook, stirring occasionally, for 4 minutes. Add the bell pepper and zucchini and cook for another 4 minutes. Remove and discard the garlic.

2. Transfer the vegetables to a large bowl and add the tomatoes, basil leaves, and pasta. Drizzle with oil, season to taste, and mix to combine. Refrigerate for at least 1 hour before serving.

NEAPOLITAN FRITTATINE

SERVES: 2
PREP: 75 MINS
COOK: 20 MINS

INGREDIENTS

10½ ounces (300g) cooked bucatini, chopped

2 tablespoons grated Parmesan cheese

½ quantity of Béchamel Sauce (page 157)

½ cup (60g) frozen peas, blanched in salted water

2 ounces (60g) prosciutto, diced

2 ounces (60g) mozzarella, drained and cubed

4 tablespoons fresh breadcrumbs

1 egg, lightly beaten

2 cups (500ml) sunflower oil

salt and pepper

Italian cuisine is full of ideas to reuse leftovers, and a delicious example are these frittatine from Naples. Here, I've used leftover bucatini and béchamel sauce.

1. Line a large baking sheet with baking parchment.

2. Mix the pasta, Parmesan, and béchamel sauce together in a large bowl. Season to taste. Mix the peas, prosciutto, and mozzarella together in another bowl.

3. Take a small handful of pasta and create a hole with your finger in the center. Insert a spoonful of the pea mixture, then seal the hole and push the mixture into a 3¼-inch (8cm) metal ring. Place the frittatine on the baking sheet and repeat with the remaining pasta and filling mixture. Refrigerate for 1 hour.

4. Place the breadcrumbs on a tray. Dip each frittatina into the egg to coat well, then dip into the breadcrumbs making sure all sides are coated. Repeat the process to coat all the frittatine.

5. Heat the oil in a large, deep skillet. Cook two at a time, for 3 minutes on each side. Drain on paper towels and serve.

INDEX

ACKNOWLEDGMENTS

A huge thank you to Catie Ziller, who gave me the opportunity to write this book; it's an honor sharing my endless love for pasta. Always grateful to Lisa for her ability to capture food at its most beautiful, and to the magic team: Michelle and Kathy. Thanks to my family, my husband Salvatore, and my children Andrea, Luca, and Mario for never abandoning their enthusiasm for another plate of pasta.

Hardie Grant North America
2912 Telegraph Ave
Berkeley, CA 94705
hardiegrant.com

Text © 2025 by Giovanna Torrico
Photographs © 2025 by Lisa Linder
Illustrations © 2025 by Michelle Tilly

Published in the United States by Hardie Grant North America, an imprint of Hardie Grant Publishing Pty Ltd.

Library of Congress Cataloging-in-Publication Data is available upon request
ISBN: 9781958417805
eBook ISBN: 9781958417812

Acquisitions Editor: Catie Ziller
Photographer: Lisa Linder
Food and props styling: Giovanna Torrico
Designer: Michelle Tilly
Copy Editor: Kathy Steer

Printed in China
FIRST EDITION

Hardie Grant

NORTH AMERICA